LIVING FULLY

LIVING FULLY

Dare to Step into Your Most Vibrant Life

MALLORY ERVIN

FOREWORD BY JAMIE KERN LIMA

CONVERGENT
NEW YORK

Published in the United States by Convergent Books,
an imprint of Random House, a division of
Penguin Random House LLC, New York.

Convergent Books is a registered trademark and its C colophon
is a trademark of Penguin Random House LLC.

Library of Congress Cataloging-in-Publication Data
Names: Ervin, Mallory, author.
Title: Living fully / Mallory Ervin.
Description: New York : Convergent, [2022]
Identifiers: LCCN 2021044412 (print) | LCCN 2021044413 (ebook) |
ISBN 9780593238332 (hardcover) | ISBN 9780593238349 (ebook)
Subjects: LCSH: Self-actualization (Psychology) | Joy. | Self-realization.
Classification: LCC BF637.S4 .E768 2022 (print) |
LCC BF637.S4 (ebook) | DDC 158.1—dc23/eng/20211006
LC record available at https://lccn.loc.gov/2021044412
LC ebook record available at https://lccn.loc.gov/2021044413

Printed in the United States of America on acid-free paper

crownpublishing.com

1st Printing

First Edition

Book design by Alexis Capitini

To my grandparents Bud and Marylyn Ervin.
The closest examples of living fully I've ever known.

FOREWORD

BY JAMIE KERN LIMA

Are you feeling the magic and miracle that is your life at this very moment? I know I'm going *there* right away, but let's start this journey off with true, transparent honesty. Right now, would you say you're truly *living fully*? Or would it be more accurate to say you want to be, but out of pure overwhelm, or exhaustion, or survival mode, you're barely feeling the day most days? Get ready, because today could be the first day of your most glorious and victorious days ahead. And to kick it off, I want you to take a moment and stop reading this book. I know that might be a surprising way to start a book, but I want you to try something. . . .

Take a moment and look around you right now. First, note what colors and textures and objects you see. And just take them in. Are the colors vibrant? Or neutral? Now, smell. What do you smell right now? Take a few deep breaths and acknowledge only what you smell. If you're in your closet trying to get some alone time to read, it might be the rug or the scent of wood or dryer sheets from the laundry. If you're in your favorite chair somewhere, maybe you smell your pet nearby or maybe it's the trash that needs to go out or the scent of your favorite cup of coffee. Just take a moment and take a deep breath in and enjoy the smell, even if it's not your favorite smell, because it's part of your glorious life.

Now I want you to pause and just listen to what you hear around you. Maybe it's absolute silence. If so, maybe you can hear your own heart beating. Or maybe you hear the noise of your kids fighting or yelling "*Mom!*" as they try to get to you. And as you hear the noise around you, pay attention to what you think about it. Is your first thought that you can never catch a break? That you just need a few minutes to yourself? Or that maybe that noise of possible annoyance could also be the noise that you cherish knowing that one day, not too many years from now, it will be the last time you have kids searching the house for you.

All moments in life are so easy to miss. So easy to assign meaning to what steals our joy, instead of multiplies it. So easy to numb away from, disassociate from, and tune out of. So easy to be so busy that we default to living in survival mode or reaction mode. In our homes, our families, our marriages, and in our own bodies. Instead of living *fully*, we're living *dully*, and we think we have to.

But what if we're simply prioritizing it all wrong. What if it's possible to actually assign meaning to, and be present for, every moment in a way that brings you joy and fills your soul? Even the hard, difficult, painful moments. What if life is happening *for* you and not *to* you?

What if God or your Creator is saying, *Hey, do you see what's around you? I gave you these senses so you could appreciate the beauty all around. Like new art that I've created to dazzle your soul each day.*

What if He is watching you right now saying, *Yeah, I know these things happening are hard and painful, but I made you with all the strength you need to overcome them, and the ability to lean on me when you can't, so that you build your trust and faith at the same time.*

What if He's watching you right now saying, *I didn't create you to numb out and get by, constantly hustling to try and accomplish the external things the world says are significant but that will never fill your soul. I created you to be a living expression of beauty and goodness and joy. I created that body you keep doubting, in the perfect image of me. I created those babies and family and friends that are challenging so you can grow into your most loving self, your deepest wisdom, and your greatest compassion.*

Nothing in your life is an accident, even the things that don't make sense to you now. They're all part of your divine destiny. But if you continue to close your eyes to the colors and textures around you because you're too busy, if you continue to miss the sweet sounds in your life making music for you right now, if you continue to attach meaning that doesn't serve you to the moments that inconvenience you, if you continue to numb out, hustle for the worthiness of others, deem busyness a badge of honor, people please into depletion, you're going to risk missing it all.

Today, right now, as you turn this next page, it's your opportunity to truly ask yourself: Are you living *dully* or are you living *fully*? See, I've learned that the most soul-filling types of *fully* are free and are accessible to us all right now, usually with a simple slight change of awareness and perspective. One that most people never step into. But I don't believe you're reading this book by accident. Maybe you've spent your life doing the best you can, but it was always with these simple things missing. Or maybe you picked it up because you have big dreams on your heart or a calling you know you've not yet stepped into because you've been too scared to go after it. Maybe today is the day you begin believing in you fully. And combined with Mallory's beautiful stories and powerful lessons in the pages to come, maybe today is the day you decide that you're going to change your life. And it's OK if you're not sure how to. Making the decision and believing it's possible is the most important first step. And I don't just *believe*, I *know* it's possible. And I'd like to finish this foreword with a prayer from me for you (as this book is for all of us, I know we might share different faiths, so please apply the word that speaks closest to you in this prayer, maybe it's God, or Creator, or Jesus, or Universe, etc.):

Dear God, I pray that the beautiful soul reading these words right now is wrapped in your loving arms as they pause, absorb, and spend some time filling up with exactly what you know they need in their life and in their soul right now. I pray that the stories and lessons on these pages speak to them in a way that helps them celebrate their own ups and downs, helps them rid themself of any shame, helps them forgive their past mistakes, helps them tune in to their glorious gifts, and helps them know that they're perfectly made. Lord, please fill them up with your Holy Spirit and open their eyes even more vividly to joy, to beauty, and to who You created them to be. Help them live love, give love, feel love, and be love. And grant them favor as they begin this journey of loving fully, giving fully, seeing their own beauty fully, tapping into their purpose and power fully, laughing fully, feeling fully, and in this one beautiful life they have, ***living fully****. In Jesus' name,* ***amen.***

Love, Jamie

Jamie Kern Lima
New York Times bestselling author of *Believe IT,*
founder of IT Cosmetics

PREFACE

I've lived quite a few different types of lives in my time on earth so far. I've lived the good girl, the addict, the public figure, the mom. I almost won Miss America, the epitome of what a polished, put-together woman looks like. And then I almost lost my life to substance abuse driven by my insatiable pursuit of perfection. I raced to the top of the Matterhorn with a television crew on my heels. And I fell to rock bottom again, burnt-out, with nothing but a broken heart and a prayer.

In none of those scenarios was I living fully. In all of them, I was running on empty.

For each of the highest highs I reached, I plummeted to the lowest low, and ultimately, I was forced to make a choice about the life I truly wanted to live. And it is that choice I made then—and continue to make every day of my life—that qualifies me to talk about living fully.

You see, I discovered that we can't find a full life in those "hero moments" just as we can't find it in the "zero moments." Instead, we find it in a practice, a constant way of life. That practice is living fully. And it leads not to a specific destination, goal, or achievement, but instead, back to the best version of yourself.

When I finally came back to myself, I realized that what had happened in my own life was probably happening to a lot of other people. It took my brokenness to have the breakthrough. I want you to have that breakthrough, only without some of the brokenness. That's why I wrote this book.

While I do consider myself the ultimate cheerleader for anyone working toward achieving their dreams, I don't want you to mistake your experience with this book as a pat on the back, a "you're worth it" type of message. We've all read those books, and we love them. But this book I wrote to be your wake-up call, the thing that turns the lights on in your life and propels you to make real change, once and for all. I want you to wake up and *stay* awake. It's so easy to look in the mirror and say out loud, "I believe I deserve to live fully," but if your actions don't reflect that belief, it's empty. It stops right there at the mirror, and far short of actual change.

So, I want you to first know you deserve it, and then act like you deserve it as you're living each day.

I didn't write this book from the top of a mountain; I wrote it with my life looking a lot more ordinary. I'm a wife and mother of two, building a business and a family. My life is drastically different and so much better than it was during all of my over-the-top moments. I actually couldn't master the art of finding fulfillment until I stopped doing all those things.

People often believe they want those big experiences because they think that's where the full life exists—they think they'll finally feel alive when they accomplish something huge. But that's simply not true. Filling my life with those big experiences—the titles and achievements—it led to emptiness. What I learned is there's an alternate route to fullness—and the actual journey to get there can feel like you've already arrived. Now I'm no longer in pursuit of big things but a big life.

I walked in a lot of shoes on my journey. Some gave me blisters, some twisted my ankles, some made me feel taller and more confident, some weighed me down, but looking at them all in my closet now, the lessons of walking a million miles in them are so clear to me. These chapters are the lessons I've learned—my lightbulb moments—and my definition of what it means to live fully.

But living fully means making some changes. Change can be scary, especially for those of us who feel like things are okay. It's natural to fear something different. You might feel fear rising in you right now because you don't want to do the work to change your life or because you're comfortable just as you are now. But what if that fear was the only thing standing in your way? What if that fear was the only thing keeping you from living more fulfilled? The good news is, you don't have to hit pause on your life to completely overhaul it. Living fully is very much something you can do while living your everyday life.

My hope is that you are able to see how fear, worry, complacency, or just a tendency to focus on things that don't really matter in the big scheme of things might be holding you back. And more important, how you hold the power to overcome them. Fearing adversity and avoiding pain is a habit of our culture that I've become determined to break in my own life—by living not in avoidance of pain but in the pursuit of things that often include it.

Whatever story you've been telling yourself about the life you "weren't handed," or the life you "don't have access to," or that you "can't afford," or that you "aren't smart enough" to achieve, or "motivated enough" to earn, I want you to know that you have the power to rewrite that story. I know this because I rewrote my own story. And in the process of rewriting my own story I was able to wake up out of a twilight existence and step into a bright new beginning.

When I think about this book and how I hope you will use it, I see myself as your guide, not as an influencer. I'm not trying to sway you or convince you; instead, I want to first help you wake up to the thrilling realization that there's a much more elevated version of this life available to you, and then to guide you toward that life in ways that are soul-stirring and livable, and that will ultimately ignite a new fire within you.

No matter where you're starting from today, *Living Fully* is for you if . . .

. . . you feel like you're on cruise control, where everything is "fine" but there's a voice inside saying you want more out of life.

. . . you wish you could bounce back faster from unexpected challenges.

. . . you feel stuck somehow, but fear is keeping you from taking a chance on something bigger, better, or new.

. . . your life feels out of balance, and you have started to lose touch with what matters to you the very most.

. . . you feel like who you are on the inside is totally mismatched with the life you're living on the outside, and you're disconnected from your true essence.

. . . you are rushing through the to-do list of life so fast that you don't get to experience true joy.

. . . you know you don't want to arrive at the end of your life and wonder what kind of legacy you are leaving behind.

I know you have the power to reengage with your life, and you know it too, deep down, or you would have tuned out that little voice inside your head saying to open this book. Whatever mysterious or curious way you have arrived at this moment, don't waste it.

To live a life is a gift we are given.

To live a full life is a gift we give ourselves.

CONTENTS

PART III: LIVING FULLY

WHO AM I WITHOUT ALL THIS?

As the hairdresser reached into my hair and slowly pulled out the final blond extension, my hands began to tremble. I knew it was crazy that I could have possibly become emotionally attached to hair extensions, but I had not gone a single day without them for more than a decade. They'd become part of my identity. I'd built a life within which my appearance played a key role, and I honestly didn't know who I was without that piece. I'd been known to spend upwards of eleven hours in a salon having old extensions removed and new ones put in, but this visit was very different. Today, these sticky chunks of fake hair, barely still clinging to my actual hair, were coming out, but nothing new was being added in. I'd be walking out of there all me, without a shred of glam. And glam had been my baseline for as long as I could recall, so *this* was going to feel downright bizarre.

When the hairdresser finally freed those last strands of fake hair and set them on the small silver table next to me, I stared blankly at my reflection in the mirror. My dark brown roots were four inches long, and my hair was all different lengths from where some of it had gotten pulled out or broken off with the extensions. My face was puffy, and I wasn't wearing a stitch of makeup. I didn't know that person gazing back at me in the mirror. Worse, I wasn't sure I *wanted* to know that person.

Snapping me out of my inner torment, the hairdresser said, "You wanted highlights too, right?" I nodded and faked a smile. I figured if my hair was going to be short and thin, it might as well still be blond.

As she started the color mixing process, I squirmed a bit as I eyed the time. I only had a short window to work with; the treatment center had strict rules about how long I could be gone, and I was not about to risk being late. It'd taken weeks to be allowed to leave at all, and in forty-five minutes, a white van with the facility name on the side was going to be waiting for me out front. I said a little prayer and then closed my eyes.

My mind was suddenly awash with memories; they flooded in as if a dam had broken. I thought of a desperate phone call to my mom in the final hours leading up to the Miss Kentucky pageant in 2009. "I don't know if I can do this, Mom. I don't know if I'm even supposed to be doing this," I'd said through tears. Then the strengthening current took me into a more recent moment when my boyfriend (now my husband) had uttered the words, "Mallory, how am I supposed to marry you? I can't do this anymore." Sinking into the emotion of that moment, I blinked—and—*bam*—I was in Varanasi, India, taping *The Amazing Race*, sleeping on the ground next to my dad between two Harlem Globetrotters, a couple of cowboys, a beggar, and his son, overwhelmed by a deep sense of gratitude and the hair-raising thrill of adventure. This uncontrollable stream of consciousness continued to rush, thrashing me over one extreme emotion after another, the highs and lows I'd experienced all mixing together and creating an ever-rising tide.

I felt my body begin to twist, and I opened my eyes to find the hairdresser nervously turning my chair around to face the mirror. I gasped. I didn't know how it was possible, but my appearance had gone from borderline to bizarre. What little was left of my hair was fried to a crisp, and the color was bright orange with white streaks. I looked like something out of a horror movie. "I-I can fix it! It just needs some toner, I think," she stammered as she saw me choking back tears. I held up my hand in silent surrender. "It's okay. I have to go," I replied as I gathered my purse and made my way to the reception desk. Still forcing back tears, I climbed into the waiting van and rode silently the entire way back to the facility.

As soon as I got back to my room, I collapsed into bed and sobbed. If ever I was going to leave treatment, it was going to be in that moment. And I got really close.

THE GOOD GIRL

"How on earth did I end up here?" I wondered aloud in between bouts of full-on ugly crying. *Who was that monster staring back at me in the mirror?* Just a few short years ago, I had been standing onstage as runner-up in the Miss America pageant. That was just one of many titles I had been clinging to for dear life. Now, after a little over a month here, I felt like a nobody. Stripped down to the barest version of myself, average, alone, I felt like no one would ever want to be around me. I believed that no one, including myself, would ever accept me in this state. I felt like I wanted to die.

The few years leading up to being forced to seek professional help had been wild, to say the least. I'd been running at top speed twenty-four hours a day. Besides my pageant stint, I'd appeared on *The Amazing Race* three times (one of those seasons was airing while I was in treatment, though I wasn't allowed to talk about it), and I had been around the world taping pilots for travel shows. To look at me, it seemed I was in the prime of my life living out a fairy tale. But I was hiding a dark secret from everyone. Underneath that glamorous, put-together exterior was a numbed-out, emotionally crippled perfectionist who was literally dying trying to outdo herself.

I'd always been a "good girl" in my early life, never tempted by drugs or alcohol. But in college, I had discovered that many kids my age dabbled in prescription medications—not always for their intended purposes. It seemed as if those who took them were able to power through anything with their endless energy, and this was very appealing to me.

So, just to see what the hype was all about, I tried it for myself. And it felt like a fire lit up in my brain. Everything came into sharp focus, and my energy shot through the roof. After taking it here and there, I wanted more. I got my own prescription by convincing a doctor I needed it, but shortly after, I started having trouble sleeping. So, I went back to my doctor for help with my new insomnia problem. He prescribed sleeping pills, and just like that, I was on the pharmaceutical seesaw of uppers and downers. I convinced myself that since a doctor had given these medications to me, it was all okay. But it wasn't. It was very far from it.

Now, I want to pause here and make something really clear. I realize that medications prescribed for mental health challenges such as attention deficit disorder, anxiety, or depression can be absolutely life-changing and even lifesaving for many people. I am in no way saying that there is anything wrong with taking prescriptions as directed by a doctor. In my case, I used prescription stimulants for a condition I didn't have, and prescription sleeping pills as a way to come down from the stimulants. And to deal with how these drugs made me feel, I'd drink a whole bottle of wine before bed every night. Probably not exactly what my physicians had in mind.

This went on for five years. The result was a total physical and emotional collapse. I may have been in my midtwenties, but my doctors told me I was already at high risk of stroke, and my blood pressure was off the charts. I was taking enough medication to kill a cow, so it's not surprising that my body was falling apart from the inside out. My hair started to fall out, my skin felt like it was crawling, my pupils were the size of my whole eyeball, I weighed under one hundred pounds, and I couldn't feel the ends of my fingers or toes. What had started as a flame of nonstop energy had become a wildfire, threatening to burn my whole life down. I hated how I felt, and I'd often find myself in church lighting candles and begging God to take away the pain and despair. I'd get on my knees on the cold altar and just beg for something to change in me.

In addition to my growing dependency on medication, I was lost in every way that a person can be lost. I was paralyzed by stress and fear, constantly obsessing about trying to top the last thing I'd done, with nothing to anchor me down. And eventually I was jobless, broke, paranoid, and spinning out of control.

I was left with two choices. I could keep doing what I was doing, which I knew was a path that would undoubtedly lead to death—honestly, within weeks, I believe, looking back—or I could get the help that those around me realized I needed. I had become a radically different person, so it was obvious to everyone on the outside that I needed help. And I needed it fast.

It was my family who worked to figure out what I was dealing with and what to do about it. When they realized I was struggling with an addiction, they researched treatment facilities and found one that seemed it would be a good place for me. Then they sat me down and told me that it was my decision, but they strongly encouraged me to agree to go.

It really was a life-or-death decision, but the choice was still not an easy one for me. Isn't it ironic how we can struggle so much with a decision like that, even when the answer is as clear as day to everyone else? Now, looking back, I can see that God answered my prayers when I let my parents take me to treatment.

A CHOICE THAT CHANGED IT ALL

So, on that pivotal night spent crying in my bed after the hair disaster, I realized I had another choice to make—one that seemed much harder than the decision to go to treatment in the first place. But it turned out to be one that would ultimately change my path forever and lead me to my life's work. And it is something I've now come to understand (after years of self-reflection): the issue that manifests is rarely ever the *actual* problem. There is usually an underlying cause that's not being addressed. The problem wasn't the substances; the problem also wasn't the hair . . . or the boyfriend, the titles, the success and notoriety, the need for approval, or anything else. The problem—*my* problem—was my *attachment* to all those things.

Just like those extensions were all tangled up and damaging my real hair, so too had my external attachments been damaging me . . . until ultimately, I got lost amidst them. I was allowing those things to become who I was. By giving them so much control, they had crept in and suffocated my spirit, leaving me empty. I mean, the fact that I literally hit the lowest of lows and wanted to *die* simply because my hair extensions were gone is a pretty strong clue that I had some deeply rooted attachments going on. It was no wonder I had spiraled into oblivion. The wildfire surrounding the drugs was what got me into treatment, but I had to work on what caused that blaze in the first place.

So, back to the choice I had to make that day: I could either continue to let go of all the unhealthy attachments I'd formed and force myself to go through the process of uncovering my own authenticity, or I could dig in my heels and refuse to proceed. As my parents, three younger siblings, and twenty-three first cousins I grew up with will tell you, I can be pretty headstrong. It was a very real possibility that I was going to walk away from treatment and try to just figure it all out on my own. I didn't know exactly what was on the other side of this, or why I had to seemingly give up everything that felt like *me*, but I chose to have faith that one day it would all make sense. So I stayed. For four more months I pried myself free from the chains I'd been clinging to for dear life.

I've since come to understand unhealthy attachments don't happen overnight; in my case, the process was years in the making. Starting at a young age, I had talent as a singer, and I was a natural achiever. I was the valedictorian of my class, I'd constantly been in that achieving mode, and frankly, I had really liked achieving. I was a happy child, and my youth was a bright and vivacious time. But there came a point, as I experienced more and more success, that I got way out of balance. I became so deeply attached to my achievements in my teens and twenties that I'd lost all semblance of myself without them. If I was ever going to fight my way back to the light—back to myself—I had to first lose my attachments to the external things I'd been clinging to.

Years later, when I was able to look back on all of it with some objectivity, I was—and continue to be—astounded and humbled at the opportunity the experience afforded me. I have lived two radically different lives.

These days, when I share something online about the darker times in my life, I'm always amazed at the overwhelming feedback I receive. It makes me realize just how many other people are living like I was, often without even knowing it. It's so easy to distract ourselves from our actual feelings, to numb out in order to avoid pain, and then to become just a passenger in our own lives.

I've also discovered that we are all searching for that comforting feeling of knowing someone else has been steeped in the darkness, and found their way back to the light, and back to themselves.

That's why it is my deepest desire and truest purpose to bare it all, to be vulnerable, to share every part of my journey so that others can benefit. I want to shout from the rooftops for the world to hear the truths I've had to learn, because they apply to all of us. But we must be willing to search within ourselves to discover what lies beneath, what wisdom we have gained or perhaps forgotten, and what we can learn from our experiences both good and bad. And that searching has to be *intentional*. Life moves at such a furious pace, and we have so many distractions coming from all angles, a constant chatter both externally and inside the echoing corridors of our mind. When we do sit down to sort out the details, it can feel too hard to hear ourselves think above the uproar of thoughts in our heads.

Maybe you've experienced this before when you've tried to write in a journal, meditate, or ponder your past and envision your future. It can be overwhelming. So you step away from it and venture back into the commotion of life, allowing the prevailing current to direct your course or worse, the undertow to pull you under.

That's because we don't really know what we know, unless we *purposely* go within and uncover the lessons and wisdom we have gained along the way in our lives.

And my goal is to guide you to purposely seek out the

answers you're looking for. Now that I have found my purpose, I get out of bed every day with both feet on the ground, ready to live my best life. It is messy, joyous, and yes, chaotic at times. But I love it and wouldn't have it any other way. I am living fully, and I can't wait to help you do the same.

PART I

The Wake-Up Call

CHAPTER 1

Amazing (G)Race

Losing is something I used to hate. I would recoil at the thought of coming in second or third—*any*thing but first. I would do anything not to lose a competition, a boyfriend, a board game, you name it. I would nearly die of overexertion, pushing myself beyond the point of just giving it my best shot. And I never lost . . . until I started losing everything.

In 2010, I was two years out of college and I had just lost Miss America. Barely—I was runner-up. Soon after, a casting person approached me and asked if I'd be interested in reality TV, specifically the show *Survivor.* I thought, *I've been starving to death for this pageant for months, and I will literally die if I do* Survivor. I graciously declined.

I thought about it a little more, and while I couldn't talk myself into the whole deserted island starvation thing, I did want a new, big goal. Before I could think another thought, the casting person called me back and asked me if I'd be interested in *The Amazing Race* instead. I stopped dead in my tracks; I was very interested in that show. In case you don't know, *The*

Amazing Race is a popular reality TV show where two-member teams competed against one another to win clues that led them on a race around the world for a $1 million prize. My dad and I had been watching it religiously for years. (We *love* it.) So, before I could even fully form the thought, I heard myself asking, "Do you think my dad could be my partner?" And that's how we ended up going on *The Amazing Race* the *first* time.

NEAR MISSES

As the oldest of four children, one-on-one time with my dad was sacred to me, so I was thrilled at the prospect of getting to spend a lot of time with him on the show. My dad is a humble, salt of the earth type of man, and I'm, well, a little loud. And since the show's contestants narrate it—there's no written script—our differing personalities really stuck out on camera. The producers let us know that while we were filming, we needed to say everything we were thinking and then some, to let the audience in on what was going on in our heads. In order to be cast for the show, they had to see the balance in our banter and initially, there was a lot more of me and not quite enough of my dad.

"Um, if we can get about seventy-five percent less of you and seventy-five percent more of him, I think you'll have a shot of making it on" was the general sentiment. We took their direction; I didn't utter every thought I had, and my dad for the first time in his life seemed to vocalize what he was thinking versus just sitting back. We found our balance, and soon we were off and running . . . literally around the world.

We didn't have much time to train and prepare for that first season, but we did as much as we could in the few weeks we had. The two things that you could do to ensure some success were to get in good physical shape and to correctly pack your backpack. We got to bring one backpack each, filled with all the supplies and clothing we might need in a race around the world.

That means I had to pack into one bag all the gear I would need for bone-chilling conditions at the top of a snowcapped mountain as well as for the hottest deserts on the planet. And I had to carry it all on my back. It's kind of like real life. You want to be prepared for every condition you could encounter but knowing that what you carry will weigh you down if it's too much. I've learned to always choose wisely what I carry with me.

I'll never forget my dad sawing off the ends of my Bobbi Brown makeup brushes in our garage with a handsaw. He didn't want me to weigh my pack down with makeup, but the few pieces he allowed required brushes. "Dad, those are good brushes. Why are you ruining them?" I yelled.

"Too heavy," he said without looking up, and continued. "Why is Whitney Houston's husband making makeup brushes anyway?" Ugh. Dads. Those two backpacks took us everywhere. Mine weighed 11.8 pounds, my dad's 22.7.

We started in England, where we competed against other teams in classic medieval competitions. We had to catapult watermelons toward targets, and one person was even hit square in the face. *Side note:* if you haven't seen this viral moment, Google "watermelon to the face Amazing Race."

Then we were on to Ghana, where we sold sunglasses as street vendors and learned a game alongside schoolchildren where we rolled a bicycle rim the distance of a field using only a stick, all in over-one-hundred-degree heat.

Next up, we raced through Norway and Sweden. We rappelled off bridges, went dogsledding through the snow while capturing flags from tree branches, and hauled enormous blocks of ice in Sweden's famous ice hotel. We rode bikes across European landscapes while remembering combinations we'd learned in other countries to unlock information about where to head next. Then we went on to plant potatoes in St. Petersburg with elderly Russian women—*after* juggling with actual clowns and sifting through filmstrips in a historic cinematography museum. And that was only half of the season.

Finally, we came to the eighth of twelve total legs of the race. Racing to the Middle East, we landed in Oman with a map and a plan, and we were on our way. In case you didn't know, on *The Amazing Race*, we didn't have phones, which means we had to rely either on the locals for directions or on maps we bought at gas stations or airports with our small daily stipend.

My dad and I started on the route our map showed, but then we saw the rest of the teams pulling off in a different direction. One of the groups we had alliances with yelled out the window to follow them, but we could see on the map that there was a shortcut, so we went with our gut. Well, there might have been a shortcut under normal circumstances, but due to a flash flood the week before, the road was completely washed out. We drove across the country for three hours in the wrong direction, only to have to turn around and spend another three hours just to get back to the place where we'd started.

We were hours behind the rest of the teams but we ended up making up time in the challenges that they took a little longer to complete. But still, it wasn't enough. We lost that leg only by the skin of our teeth, but we did lose, and therefore were eliminated from that season of the show. But we really were amazing racers. (No pun intended.) We knew we were better than that; after being eliminated so late in the race, we had a gnawing sense of longing for another chance.

Three weeks after we got home, my phone rang. It was the head of casting asking us to return to appear on an all-star season. *OMG. What?* Before we knew it, we were off again, already filming another season before the first one even aired.

Because we lost, we were getting to race around the world on our favorite show . . . *twice*. We couldn't believe it.

That second season had us immediately diving with great white sharks in Sydney harbor, racing through the outback in kangaroo suits, tasting teas in Guangzhou that we then had to identify in Calcutta, making chocolate in Switzerland, and getting dropped out of helicopters onto some of the largest mountains in the world. We learned to dance the samba with Brazilians and make caipirinhas on a Copacabana beach. We dug through mud and frog pits to find clues in Japan and rode yaks through the foothills of China.

And then there we were—we had made it to the last leg. We were in Miami, Florida, and all we had to do was get to the finish line in order to win one million dollars. We were running at full speed from our airplane Jetway to jump into a cab, and just as my dad was reaching for the door handle, a woman came out of nowhere and yelled, "Hey! I've been waiting for this taxi!" Our hearts were pounding, the clock was ticking, and there was a million-dollar prize on the line. But we did the same thing we would have always done and let her have the cab.

Thinking nothing of it, we jumped in the next taxi that pulled up. The only problem was the driver didn't speak English and didn't know how to get around Miami, so we got lost for two hours, which put us hours behind the rest of the teams. We pushed through and tried to not give up hope. Eventually we did make it—and when we showed up at the final challenge, which was connecting water and electricity in a mobile home, the other teams were shocked because they hadn't seen us since we ran off the plane. My dad hooked up that mobile home faster than even the challenge testers did. Everyone was floored. It was our attempt at a Hail Mary, but still not enough. The other teams had arrived so far ahead of us that it just wasn't possible to win, even though we finished the challenge in a fraction of the time it took the others.

We ended up losing *The Amazing Race* again, and by only one minute and thirty seconds.

THE UNEXPECTED NO

Sounds like a heartbreaker, doesn't it? Well, it was . . . in the moment. But looking back, here's why it was the best thing that could have happened to me. During that time in my life, the pageants, the racing around the world, the notoriety, all of it, I had become a numbed-out, empty shell of myself. I was quickly approaching the abyss, and honestly, if we'd won, and I'd had all that money in my bank account, I'm pretty sure I would have wound up dead. Of course, I didn't realize it at the time, but a million dollars would have been the very worst thing for me. I was teetering on the edge of a full-blown prescription pill addiction, and more money would have meant more idle time, and that would have only cleared a path for that wildfire to burn faster. There are times in our lives when the unexpected no is the exact right answer.

If it were not for the woman who stole our taxi, I may never have known what it is to live fully, and I surely wouldn't be writing this book today. Up until the point of losing *The Amazing Race*, not once but twice (and eventually three times), losing wasn't something I did gracefully. But now it is. I am so thankful for the Amazing Grace God gave me in losing *The Amazing Race*.

We don't always know exactly why something doesn't work out, but what I've come to realize is the sooner we can accept there's an unexpected and unpredictable reason for it, the sooner we can move into the fullness of something new. Those moments can be pivotal catalysts for change. They could be saving your life. It could be that the thing you thought you wanted and needed most in this world was not meant to happen.

Sometimes we can convince ourselves so strongly that we *need* what we *want*. But many times, these two things are not connected, no matter how connected we feel to a desire. When I think back on the things I needed in life, they did not always come to me the way I wanted. They were, instead, delivered to me by grace, something beyond my control.

You may not have seen a finish line on a national competition show; your finish line may look a lot different. But it doesn't matter. It's that tangible or intangible point you've been setting your sights on, and that you're certain will bring you fulfillment. What a gift it is when we're handed what we didn't know we actually needed.

I imagine you can think of times in your life when the unexpected no, the loss of something you thought you needed so desperately, turned out to be the best possible outcome for you. So, the next time you're faced with having to let go of something you thought was going to lead to happiness, ask yourself if this is one of those times. Take a look around and see if perhaps there's a reason why it's better to *not* cross that finish line first. To *not* win. To *not* reach that particular goal. The more open you are to seeing that this is actually grace in action in your life, the more likely you will be able to understand where it's leading you instead. And you may just get a better opportunity like I did. You just have to be open to it.

I've been blind, fumbling around in the darkness many times, but every time, it is Amazing Grace that helps me see what a full life truly looks like for me. I spent years mourning the things I thought I wanted, but looking back, I can see the loss of those things as moments of grace. Just like the hymn says, I was blind but now I see.

CHAPTER 2

Relighting the Fireworks

"Did you say Malta?" I asked, with my phone pinned between my ear and my shoulder as I frantically (and as quietly as possible) typed M-A-L-T-A into the Google search bar. In the seconds between when I asked the question to the person on the other end of the line and his response, my eyes scanned the search results, map, and photos that popped up on my laptop's screen.

"Yes, you've heard of it?" he asked.

"Uh, yes, I have! Well, recently, but yes. It looks beautiful." I had been in that part of the world before, so I felt relatively confident in my answer.

"Well, we think it's a perfect location for a travel show pilot. And we were actually wondering if you'd be interested in hearing more about hosting the show, or if you'd have time for something like that. . . ." Of course I had the time. At that point in my life, I had nothing but time.

"Sure!"

"'Sure' you'll do it or 'sure' you'll talk about it more?"

"Sure, both. I'll do it." And just like that, after a few more logistics were in place, I was on my way to Malta.

At twenty-four years old, with two seasons of *The Amazing Race* under my belt, my pageant days behind me, and a growing dependency on prescription medications, I would have done almost anything to feel relevant in some way again, so an incredible chance like this, I didn't even need to think about it. I thought it was the answer to my prayers. And it was, but in a very different way than I expected.

You see, I'd spent a lot of time kneeling on church floors up until that phone call. Alone, in the dark, my hands and forearms mashed against the cold concrete. That shocking feeling of the cold against my reaching arms sometimes felt as though my body was literally rejecting solid ground, or sound guidance. I felt like someone had shut the lights off inside of me. I felt nothing and everything all at the same time. They were some of my darkest days.

The only light I found was in the church, but alone. Always alone. I was certainly not ready for others to see that my light had been extinguished. I was even embarrassed for God to see it sometimes. I would start my prayers with "Sorry, you gave me everything and . . . just sorry. Help me . . . can you help me? Please." I knew something was wrong. I felt like I was wandering around in a pitch-black room searching for a light switch. I could have wasted the rest of my days on earth doing that, and not even lived to find the switch again.

And then, this opportunity came along.

I see now that God had begun the process of answering my prayer the moment I got that call. Because He knew that, first and foremost, He needed to remind me of the light that lived within me. And He knew I had to be taken out of my current circumstances to help me to see it.

The show was to be called *Mallory Meets Locals*, and the plan was for me to travel all over the tiny country of Malta, meeting local people from all different walks of life and living alongside them—trying my hand at their crafts, getting to know their stories, and seeing this beautiful country through their eyes. This was going to be the next jewel in my crown. I was delighted.

When I got there, the show was shot all over the country and I got to sit down with dozens of people, all of whom so clearly embodied what it was to live fully. I met a baker, and I made bread with him using a stone oven that had been burning nonstop for over one hundred years, starting when his grandfather had built it with his own hands. I helped make fireworks for the annual *Festa Santa Maria*, the Feast of the Assumption of Mary, and I saw how passionate they were about creating the most awe-inspiring fireworks show imaginable. The men—grown men with jobs and families—would volunteer almost all of their free time to do this, and they would cry telling me about shows past and the fireworks they'd dreamed up and made a reality.

I learned how to make blown glass vases alongside passionate artists who saw in their minds a vision for a work of art so clearly that they *literally* breathed life into the glass. I even went fishing with a man who caught the largest shark in the world. Each day was a new adventure and a new opportunity to see someone else's light shining brightly, which allowed me to begin the process of relighting my own.

When I wasn't filming, I would wander the streets of Malta. Around every corner was beauty that stirred my soul: a breathtaking seascape, a narrow alleyway adorned with vibrant flowers overflowing from window boxes, an empty church, or one filled with seekers like me, but with real problems, not imagined ones or ones that they had created themselves. There was a vibrancy, an undeniable heartbeat to the place.

I was struck most of all by how everyone's spirits seemed to be so full, which was just so opposite of how I'd felt before I got there. I was disconnected from reality. I had allowed the stress of what came next for me to consume me, to remove me completely from my life. But the people around me were so connected to their culture, to their purpose, to their passion; meanwhile, my own passions had been burned down to a nub. Again and again, I would find myself inside one of the many gorgeous churches there. I'd sit in the pews and beg for direction, and at that time and in that place, *direction found me*.

The Power of a Change of Scenery

By getting plucked out of Nashville, Tennessee, and temporarily relocating to an entirely different country, a whole world away, I was given the ultimate gift and opportunity to leave my surroundings and reconnect with myself.

Aside from finding inspiration from my change in location, something else ended up having a significant impact on me during that trip. I slowly ran out of the prescriptions that were controlling my life, and I had no way to refill them. I started to unintentionally detox, which you'd think would make matters worse. Instead, I felt the first glimmers of myself starting to come back. It was the first time I realized that in numbing out all the bad things in my life, I was also smothering out the good.

I had forgotten that feeling . . . the feeling of myself. The feeling of joy not chemically manufactured. And once I remembered, I wondered why I had started taking the pills in the first place. I now realize it's because it happened slowly, but sometimes these things happen so gradually that we don't always catch them.

The energy and excitement throughout that summer were so intense that I could feel it deep in my bones, as if they were cracking open and being filled with new marrow. For the first time in a long time, I was fully present, fully immersed, living again. As if someone had struck a match inside me, I could feel my inner fire lighting back up.

Hide It Under a Bushel

I believed the show was going to be "it" for me, my next big achievement, and to a degree, it was. But not in the way I had first hoped. The show didn't get picked up. However, my experience in Malta showed me just how empty I was, and it inspired me on a cellular level to find my way back to my inner fire.

When it came time for me to head to the airport, I was looking out the window of the car, really sad my time there was over for now, and I saw an American flag waving over someone's house. And then another one. And another! I said to my producer and host, whose home I'd been living in, "Why are there so many American flags out?"

"They're for you, Mallory!"

Super surprised and kind of confused, I said, "Yeah, right. No, really! Why are they out?"

"You made quite the impression on everyone here. They're sad to see you go."

I was sad to go too. I didn't want to leave the people, places, and moments behind that made me feel alive.

All along the way toward the airport, I saw flag after flag and so many of my new friends waving as we drove. Here I'd spent all this time praying for signs, begging God for direction, and now—this. Tears rolled down my cheeks as awareness dawned on me that these people, who just a few short months ago had been complete strangers, seemed to love me. *Maybe*, I thought, *it was time to start loving myself again.*

Isn't it funny how we wander around aimlessly through life sometimes? Uptight, confused, we walk and walk, without a single step in an intentional direction. That is, until something reminds us of our spirit again. When we are children, it seems so easy to live with a light beaming from us, guiding us. Hide it under a bushel? No, I'm going to let it shine! Just like that. Well, it's not that easy the older we get; sadly, the bushels are *every*where. The whole world can be one huge bushel. But the problem in adulthood is that the bushel puts our lights out so slowly that we don't even realize it's happening, and then we don't remember what it looked like to live with the light on. And you can't fight for what you don't know. That's why being reminded is such a critical step in the process of living fully.

My experience in Malta did some of the "remembering" work for me. Somewhere coming off the uppers and downers, I caught a glimpse of myself again, and I was reminded of what I was like before, of what it felt like to be driven by passion again.

We're lucky if it just happens upon us like that, but most of the time, it doesn't happen this way. So often, we have to really look for the reminders. And that starts with reflecting on times in your life when you've seen and lived in the light before.

Relight Them . . . Again

The ultimate ending of the Malta story reveals a really important lesson. I came back on *fire*. I was clearheaded, passionate, full of hope, happy, feeling truly content, and bursting with life again.

Two days after returning home, I refilled my prescriptions.

What. In. The. World? It makes no sense, yet so much sense at the same time. I can see the reasons why I went straight back to the same life I'd had before I left. Nothing at home had changed. I was walking back into the same groups of people, the same problems, in the same locations. So, of course I did this.

I forgot to hold on to what I'd learned.

Don't we all? We forget so easily. This is life. One minute, we're watching a brilliant fireworks display, and the next, we're all alone in the dark. Then our job is to relight them again.

So, instead of returning to our old patterns, when we're standing at the crossroads of those significant changes in our lives, we can make a conscious choice to relight our fireworks. The next time you feel your fireworks starting to dim, think about actions you can take to help ignite and brighten them again.

Get with Your People

Who knows you well and can help you reconnect with what you truly value in life? Who can lovingly point out where you've gotten off track, or in what ways you might be keeping yourself from the life you want? As one of my favorite authors, Jen Hatmaker, writes "One of the best parts of being human is other humans. It's true, because life is hard; but people get to show up for one another, as God told us to, and we remember we are loved and seen and God is here and we are not alone. We can't deliver folks from their pits, but we can sure get in there with them until God does."* I know I've experienced this over and over in my life with my family and close friends. Showing up for one another in the pit, on the peak, and everywhere in between—that is what we are *meant* to do for one another.

Talk to your people and be honest about how you're feeling. They may be able to help you relight your spark. Choose

* Jen Hatmaker, *For the Love: Fighting for Grace in a World of Impossible Standards*, (Nashville: Nelson Books, 2015), p. xvi.

wisely the people who surround you, and your life will look *vastly* different.

FIND GRATITUDE

I once got to sit in the front row at a Tony Robbins event. Staring up at a man who lives in an elevated state almost constantly was electrifying. I could feel the energy pouring out of him. You know when you walk into the movie theater and the front-row seat is all that's left? You sit down and the movie starts, but it's almost as if you can't take it all in because it's too much happening right in front of you. It was like that. And the thing that stuck with me the most from that weekend was such a simple practice.

First, he had us place our hands on our hearts, close our eyes, and breathe in deeply. Over the span of several minutes, he prompted us to imagine experiences in our lives that we were immensely grateful for. The times in our lives where we felt overwhelmed with gratitude or peace. I instantly thought of my husband, Kyle; my children; the night I won Miss Kentucky; and nights on beach vacations grilling oysters outside with my family. Gratitude to have an experience like *The Amazing Race* and to be immersed in so many cultures. I thought of all the times in my life when I have felt deep, deep joy.

Then he had us imagine ourselves back in those moments and feel those emotions. When I did this for several minutes, everything felt different. It's like the lights were turned back on. It was a profound difference, a complete change in my state of mind.

I now do this gratitude practice frequently. And every time, the issues or dilemmas I've been dealing with look different because I've turned on the lights, so to speak, and tuned in to my deep joy around situations I'm immensely grateful for.

Have you ever noticed how when you approach hardship from a place of gratitude and hope, it changes the game completely? Gratitude is not a new concept, but it's one of the nonnegotiables to living fully.

You can meditate or think deeply on what you're thankful for and really feel a shift, or you can do another personal favorite of mine and others: the gratitude list. Maybe you've heard of or even tried a gratitude list before, but have been tempted to dismiss it. That's because sometimes tools in the self-help toolkit show up so often in various forms that they begin to lose their meaning. As a result, maybe we assume they aren't impactful, but I think the reason we hear about them so much is because they *work*.

I know firsthand that gratitude lists can be transformative, especially if practiced daily. These bright spots in your day can be just enough of a reminder to alter your thoughts and light up any darkness you might be feeling.

Changing Your Mind's Landscape vs. Your Actual One

When I feel like my life is in chaos, one of the simplest steps I can take to realign myself is to get out of my current physical space. Have you ever noticed you feel better when you get outside or shake things up? You create a new flow, and it can help shift your perspective.

You don't have to go globe-trotting in order to accomplish this. You can always make small shifts in your life with things that take you to another place, like going to the park down the street, or taking a hike, or even a long walk on the treadmill. Think of it as changing your mind's landscape versus your actual one.

Even if you don't find inspiration in movement, you can still find it outside of yourself. It can mean reading a book that will reaffirm the things you know to be true but forgot. Or maybe it's listening to a song or podcast that stirs your heart.

Whatever it is, creating your own plan is important because we all get stuck in the darkness sometimes and forget what lights us up. It's not a matter of if, but *when* we forget. It's a human thing. I just don't want you to spend your life wandering around, searching high and low for the light switch by yourself in the same old house. There are easier ways to relight your spark.

CHAPTER 3

The Cover-Up

"Helloooo," I yelled into a dusty, long-since-closed antiques shop off the side of the road in the middle of nowhere, Kentucky. It was one of those hellos like I wanted to see if anyone was there, but I didn't really want an answer. I wasn't doing well with people at that point in my life. My active addiction was making everyday encounters hard for me. I stood there in a red dress and little brown boots, looking put-together enough to keep the world from worrying about me, but that red dress might as well have been a red flag because things were so not okay. I was twenty-eight and my life was in shambles.

The door was wide open and the place had clearly been abandoned. There was a Closed sign knocked over on its side, and the front yard was a mess with random stuff. I had spiraled into a weird obsession with junk, which I referred to as "vintage." Fancying myself some sort of American Picker, I would pile all kinds of stuff—old furniture, books, clothing, and more—into my life, into my garage, into my home, into my parents' home. Looking back, it's so obvious to me the things my subconscious mind was doing when it was out of control. When we aren't dealing with our problems, they manifest into the light of day, for all the world to see.

I crept into that dirty space and started turning things over, looking at them, breathing in the heavy dirt that was flying through the air and swatting cobwebs and old debris away, completely locked in on this junk. I tore through the items around me, wondering what I could fit into my car, what I could shove into my life, anything I could use to cover up my pain. My life looked a lot like this store did—once full of dreams and coveted things, all forgotten and left behind, and then someone shut off the lights.

Breathless with anticipation (obsession), I took a few more steps inside the store and all at once, *crash*—my legs literally fell through the floor. There I was, alone, out of my mind and now halfway through the floor of a pitch-dark abandoned building off the side of a road in Kentucky. My phone was in my car, which was parked, unlocked, outside the store with the door wide open. There's a little glimpse into how my mind used to work back then.

It took me about thirty minutes to crawl out. I had fallen at least six feet, and it would've been farther except for the pile of junk on the floor below that broke my fall. It was pitch-black, and I had to find and stack three huge rubber tires to hoist myself back up to solid ground. When I finally pulled myself free, I sat down on a filthy old table and inspected the damage to my legs. These were not simply superficial scrapes. I was legitimately bleeding, like free-flowing blood running down both of my spray-tanned legs. Any sane person would have sought medical attention. But, no. Standing there, coughing and sweating, I dusted my legs off and . . . *kept going*. You might think that falling through the floor would have given me pause, perhaps shaken me enough to reevaluate what exactly I was doing there. But again, no. The threat of tetanus was no match for the tenacity with which I was collecting stuff to bury my problems.

An old man eventually emerged and looked at me like I was crazy (which I was), and once I'd assured him I was all right, he told me his daughter and her friend had started some project and abandoned it and moved back to California. He said, "Take whatever you want. I don't care." Turns out, the city had condemned the building and told him to doze it down or they would.

You would have thought I won the lottery. I *needed* this junk.

When I arrived back at my condo, my legs crusted with blood, I opened the trunk of my car. For a brief second, I saw the contents for what they were—cobweb-covered and dirt-encrusted *garbage*. Tables, stools, old jewelry, and a thousand other knickknacks were jammed together, taking up all the available space. You see, my logical mind knew the truth all along that it was junk. But I was so desperate to distract myself from what was going on in my head that I didn't care. I chose to see this as a productive habit, a cool hobby that made me seem deep and thoughtful.

This odd, obsessive habit followed me everywhere for a long time. I would smuggle home bags of seashells from exotic beaches, and then make my friends string them into bracelets I never wore. I'd regularly visit vintage stores in my hometown, hauling home stacks of doilies and tarnished jewelry that just ended up collecting dust in my childhood room. I'd frequent church bookstores and buy thirty-five-cent books by the box, never opening one. I was well on my way to becoming a legitimate hoarder.

The fact was, my mind so badly needed to deal with all the emotional clutter I'd been ignoring that it manifested into this hoarding obsession. I was avoiding, avoiding, avoiding the truth, and this junk was a way to distract me from it. But at some point, I was going to have to start dealing with my problems, or else I was going to suffocate underneath the physical and metaphorical weight of the trash I'd dragged into my life. The chaotic mess I was creating on the outside perfectly matched the chaos of undealt-with issues that were mounting up inside of me. I knew that facing those issues would be hard, it would be painful, and so I did anything to avoid them. I now know avoidance plays out in any number of strange ways in our lives, but it never leads us anywhere we want to go.

Nowhere to Go, Nowhere to Grow

Pain avoidance is a powerful motivator for mediocrity. It keeps us stuck or going in circles. How can you truly thrive if you are constantly sidestepping anything that might touch a nerve? Avoiding things outside of your comfort zone because something similar has caused you pain in the past can prevent you from experiencing the richness of all life has to offer. And in the long run, it can make the things you are avoiding or repressing much, much worse. I think the fear of pain is the brush we often use to paint ourselves right into a corner, nowhere to go, nowhere to grow. And that's exactly where I ended up—in a corner, under a mountain of useless, dusty old junk.

In my case, the issues I'd been frantically trying to ignore and cover up had to do with my addiction that had sped off the rails like a runaway train along with my obsessive need to be seen as succeeding in ways the world could see. For you, it might be other uncomfortable truths that you haven't been willing to face. Maybe it's money, your health, a relationship you're not meant to be in, guilt you've been carrying around like a hundred-pound weight, depression, a low-grade yet constant case of anxiety, or something else. As much as we wish these things would just go away, if we smother them with distractions, they won't. In fact, trying to avoid them can strengthen them and give them strange powers to creep into our lives from all kinds of odd angles. It's no secret that suppressing our emotions can even result in physical ailments, threatening to damage our long-term health.* It is far better to face them than to avoid or suppress them. Our subconscious mind is super clever, and it will just keep bringing these things to the surface in unexpected ways until they choke the life out of you or until you finally face them. Trying to bury them deep in our psyche is a *life destroyer*.

During this phase of my life, I was repressing my emotions, avoiding them instead of facing them head-on. Feeling frustrated? Cover it up. Feeling rejected? Bottle that. Resentful and angry, even fearful? Oh, for sure cover that right up. I was all smiles on the outside while screaming on the inside. And I used a plethora of methods to cover these things up; they ranged from bingeing television shows and scrolling social media to shopping compulsively, altering my mind with drugs or alcohol, or finding a new boyfriend—anything to feel something other than my actual emotions.

My guiding principle back then was to appear put together and keep "succeeding" forward, no matter *what*. Facing the truth would have slowed me down and for sure given away that I was not a success anymore. And the *appearance* of perfection mattered more to me than actually feeling fulfilled.

---

* Hilary Jacobs Hendel, "Ignoring Your Emotions Is Bad for Your Health. Here's What to Do About It," *Time*, February 27, 2018. https://time.com/5163576/ignoring-your-emotions-bad-for-your-health/

UNCOVERING THE TRUTH

Maybe you're like I was and the issue is as obvious as a house filled to the rafters with worthless clutter and you want to do anything but face it. And you'd like everyone else to look the other way as well. Everything's *fine*. (We'll get to that in another chapter.) Or maybe your issues are still just simmering and haven't quite escalated to that point yet, but you know good and well there are certain things you're choosing to ignore or cover up. Well, my friends, let me tell you that once I finally uncovered all that stuff, I found the light of day is a *much* friendlier setting for managing our monsters.

Much like the process of covering up, which can happen quickly and unconsciously, the process of uncovering can be surprisingly swift as well, once you get in the habit. One way we can deal with uncomfortable emotions is to look for the reasons behind those emotions. When I'm feeling a strong negative emotion like anxiety, fear, or sadness, I ask myself, "What is this really about?" If I'm wanting to avoid a social interaction, I try to get to the heart of why I don't want to go and see what it's connected to. Once I see that connection, the next time I experience that emotion, I can choose to face it rather than covering it up.

Next, I look for patterns in my life. Rather than tackling my issues one by one and seeing each one as singular, instead, I find the pattern they create. As soon as a problem arises, I think, *Has this situation come up recently?* Or, *Was I dealing with this same issue five, ten, fifteen years ago?* Then I can step back a bit and see my part in that particular persistent problem. If it keeps raising its ugly head in my life, I could be the common denominator.

Maybe you've sensed this pattern in your own life. If it's a relationship issue you seem to relive over and over, it could be that you're choosing a certain kind of person that isn't right for you. Or if it seems like you are always having problems at work, maybe you're trying to fit into a certain career that isn't aligned with your passions or values.

For me, I had a pattern that started as the slow burn of perfectionism, then turned into a deep-seated need to prove myself, and from there evolved into a full-blown obsession with how others perceived me. Had I spotted my pattern of needing outside approval earlier on, I might have been able to catch myself before I went over a cliff.

Seeing your pattern(s) is the first step. Once you make an effort to interrupt that pattern you will see a new way of living, one where you are no longer held hostage by your own emotions. And once you gain momentum, you'll start to feel a freedom that makes you feel lighter, less burdened. In fact, it does feel a bit like losing the first few pounds on a diet. You'll feel excited, inspired, and determined to continue on down a path of changing for the better.

Awareness is half the battle. Think of it as lugging around an overweight backpack full of undealt-with junk through your life. You're hauling it into relationships, into jobs, into friendships, into your parenting and every other area of your life. There isn't enough overhead space on the airplane of life to be shoving even more good-for-nothing, slow-us-down, self-sabotaging excess cargo.

And that cargo can include little things or much larger, more serious ones. The simple things are the ones we'd all rather procrastinate. You know—getting in shape, trying to improve a credit score, finishing a work or school project, and so on. Sometimes we just don't have the energy, desire, or ability to manage them, and so we tell ourselves, *I'll get to that eventually*, or *maybe if I cover my eyes, it'll go away*. We've all done it, and while we know logically that they can hold us back or loom over our lives like a suffocating haze, well, we conveniently avoid that truth too.

Now, for the more serious avoidances. Usually, they are things tied closely to pain or even trauma. We've either been hurt in the past and it's affecting our present, or we're afraid of future pain we might have to endure. I love how Glennon Doyle puts it. "Whatever we use to numb the pain hurts us more than the pain would have. Let it be. It'll pass and leave you bigger, better, kinder, softer."* I believe that's true. Numbing, covering up, or ignoring pain just creates a new set of problems, and it doesn't ever allow for the pain to pass naturally. Instead, it hangs around in the background, lurking, lingering, and threatening us. When you deal with it head-on, the pain will subside.

Take Action

Okay, so what happens once we've dragged everything out into the open air? We put things where they need to go:

- Some things we uncover and realize they can actually live alongside us, bold-faced and out in the world. Like those unfinished projects we're ready to dive back into—fixing our finances, finishing that degree, starting that business, and so on.

- Some things can go right into the trash, never to be seen or heard from again. (Ahem, I'm looking at you, mom guilt.)

- Some things might be broken, but we know we can begin to mend them. Like relationships that need some attention (say, with a significant other, or a strained mother-daughter relationship).

* Glennon Doyle, Twitter post, April 19, 2015, 11:45 a.m., https://twitter.com/glennondoyle.

- Some things may require work that we need to do with a hand from a professional, like depression, anxiety, or past trauma.

Once we've figured out where things go, we need to figure out what action we can take. Can we pick up the phone and call that person who wants to make amends? Could we make that doctor's appointment and deal with that health issue finally? Is it setting a time to have that tough conversation with our partner? Can we commit to a manageable weight loss and health goal, then take the first step by signing up for a class or finding a better routine? Maybe it's forgiving someone who hurt us so that we no longer have to carry around resentment (or maybe it is you who need to ask for forgiveness). These are all actions we can take, *immediate* actions, that will then build on each other and create a natural momentum in our quest toward living fully.

Open the Mail

When I was early in recovery, I learned the term "open the mail." It's a metaphor that represents the tiny tasks that we don't face right away because we don't want to be reminded of a larger issue at hand. We don't want to open that letter or package because we're afraid it's a notice of some bigger issue we'll have to handle. So we let it sit, unopened, and we ignore our problems (for a while). But sometimes getting the simplest tasks done—opening the mail—can completely change our mind-set. Then, once you get into the practice of facing little things head-on rather than letting them pile up in some corner of your home, you become a person who automatically opens the mail rather than avoiding it. I eventually became that person, and ultimately it freed me from an invisible prison in which I'd been slowly withering away.

Chatter Is Cheaper

I do want to put a little blip on your radar as you begin this process. It's a reaction I've seen happen many times after someone comes face-to-face with an issue they've now brought into the daylight. It's the inclination to run straight out the front door to everyone you know and talk about your issue, again and again. Before too long, our best friend, hairdresser, neighbor down the street, siblings, coworkers, and nail tech are all well aware of our problem, and they've each given their two cents on what we should do about it, but we have yet to make one move toward solving it. Why? Very often, we are doing this as yet another form of avoidance. We convince ourselves that talking in circles about it is the same as dealing with it, but I can promise you, it is not. I've done this time and again, where I've found myself talking to everyone I know about a problem, and I get caught up in a spin cycle of discussion just to avoid making the decision myself.

If you asked your spouse to take out the trash and all they did was *talk* about it—which trash cans need emptying, which is the correct bin outside, when the garbage truck is coming next—would the trash still be sitting right where it was in the kitchen ten minutes ago? It sure would, and smelling worse by the minute. Uncovering things we've been avoiding only to then sit around and talk about them is pointless. Talk is cheap, chatter is cheaper.

I know sometimes we just want to feel like we aren't alone, and to know that other people have been through similar (or worse) struggles. Validation is okay, but pick the advice you want to follow, dismiss the rest, and then get a move on. You've got a whole lot of living to do and no time to waste.

The hours and days and years I spent sorting through physical junk instead of dealing with my issues and emotions are ones I'll never get back, and ones I'll cringe at forever. But it also became energy I used to fuel my transformation. Now, when I begin obsessing over stuff or trying to cover something up, I catch myself. I know to stop and look at the truth of the situation, no matter how ugly it is, and I manage it. I want the same for you. Because I can tell you, it's amazing how much better we feel when we direct our energy into actually living our lives rather than escaping them.

CHAPTER 4

Shiny Objects

Having been a singer for my entire life, I rarely missed an opportunity to perform, so while I was in treatment, I sang at chapel every week. Family and guests were allowed to come, so it was always a full house. Chapel was a bright, hopeful spot for all of us, something we patients looked forward to. It helped us feel connected with the outside world. I didn't realize it, but those Sunday morning performances were the last vestige of my previous life that I was hanging on to. My talent differentiated me, set me apart, and (surprise) I liked how that felt.

One Monday morning, the day after a particularly meaningful chapel experience, I walked into the room where I'd be meeting with my therapist, and one of the senior directors of the entire facility was sitting there. I stopped in my tracks, thinking *What is going on here?* It felt like it was an intervention (and I guess it was, in a way). I tentatively took a seat. The director spoke first, "Mallory, I believe you're familiar with the concept of a mask, and the importance of taking off the mask in order to do the work. Right?"

For a moment, I thought maybe we were going to make papier-mâché masks or some other token self-help activity. But this mask metaphor, commonly used in treatment, refers to our public or masked persona versus our authentic selves underneath. Often, people who are in an active addiction project these outward appearances to convince those around them that nothing is wrong when, really, they are crumbling inside.

"Oh, yes. We've discussed this, and I've been working on it," I said. Didn't he realize how hard it had been to let go of pretty much every single thing that had defined me? Every outward-facing layer I had meticulously created over time had been painstakingly removed. The layers were all peeled back. I felt completely stripped-down, bare, average. Everything related to my physical appearance—gone. My hair, lashes, makeup—all of it. I got a nice little reminder of it every time I looked in the mirror and saw my broken-off Fanta-orange hair. And any mention of my previous accomplishments, including Miss America or *The Amazing Race*, was strictly off-limits too, at that point. I didn't know what more I could do to take off the mask. So, yes, I was familiar with the concept of taking off the mask.

"That's great. I'm glad to hear it. We're going to continue that work by taking a new step. You're no longer going to be singing in chapel on Sundays."

"I'm sorry, *what*?" I felt like a hot wash had just gone through my body, and I immediately got defensive. "Wait, but singing in chapel isn't even about being the center of attention. It's about hope. This is wrong. I know you think you know what you're doing here, but I'm really certain you're wrong about this."

My therapist chimed in at this point, trying to calm me down. "Mallory, we aren't trying to take anything away from you. This is so that you can continue your growth here. I know it's hard to see that now, but it's necessary."

I was crushed. I'd been singing pretty much as long as I'd been speaking. To be told by someone else, someone who was guiding my rehabilitation, that I was no longer allowed to sing? They might as well have made me invisible. I felt they were taking away my self-expression, my gift. As much as I wanted to push back, I knew I couldn't do it. Not right then anyway. I nodded, trying not to cry, and quietly replied, "Okay."

I was pretty subdued through the rest of my therapy session that day as I stewed over the decision. I just couldn't believe it. My singing was my last shiny object, the final part of me that I was proud of and that I could share with others around me. Without that, who was I? I thought, *I guess I don't want to get better because better seems worse.*

Later that evening I told my friends in treatment what had happened. I gleaned some comfort from the outrage they displayed. "What do you mean you can't sing anymore?" "That's crazy! We need it!" Before I knew it, they wrote letters to people at the top, explaining that their family members come on Sunday, and they also wanted to hear me sing. They asked how on earth this was going to help me in my recovery. Often, when we've been shut down or shut out in some way, we find someone else to fight our battles, and that's exactly what I had done. My friends' requests, no matter how well-intentioned they may have been, didn't get through, and I wasn't allowed anywhere near a microphone for most of the remainder of my time in treatment.

Looking back, that was a huge turning point for me. I think if the powers that be had not made that decision on my behalf, I may not have recovered from all my addictions. It was, as they said, *necessary*. I had already come face-to-face with my intense attachment to my appearance. That was *big* for me, and I thought that was it. But after a couple of silent

Sundays passed, I began to see that singing had been the last tiny shred of outside approval I'd been clinging to. Not singing was my first brush with the deeper work I needed to do, beyond the substances, beyond the public persona. It was yet another attachment I had been subconsciously holding on to for dear life.

I had to let it go.

What I'd been missing up to that point was just how attached I had been to *people seeing me as different, special, bright, anything but average*. That was the truth underneath all of it. I learned that we can't get well if we're still putting on any aspect of the front that we're attempting to strip away. I had to figure out how to find validation not from other people, but from within. From that moment on, my work finally became an inside job, which allowed me to create a true shift away from the need for shiny objects in my life.

The Deeper Work

When we are seeking advice or answers for how to live a better, fuller, more meaningful life, sometimes we grab on to a specific message about how to change ourselves, and then we get to work on it. For instance, we think, *Oh, I get it. I need to have more gratitude. I'll make daily gratitude lists, I'll have a gratitude jar, and I'll change my license plate to GR8FUL.* And maybe things improve incrementally. Maybe that shift into gratitude does address some of what was wrong. But then, before long, the initial impact wears off. And you stop the lists, the jar goes in a cabinet. You feel empty again, and so you look for more answers, more habits to change, more problem areas to address.

This can turn into a lifelong game of Whac-A-Mole. Those problems just keep popping up, and you keep trying to get rid of them with this or that solution. But will that process ever truly lead to living a bigger life? I don't believe so, no. Real, lasting change can occur only if we make it a transformation from the inside out. Start from scratch, get down to the foundation, and then rebuild from there.

When I first started to realize changes I needed to make, I went at it with a mentality of *I really want to fix the broken parts of the old person because I know her. That will be easier to accomplish than taking a deep dive and becoming a whole new person.* I tried hard to do that, and I even convinced myself it was working. After I let go of my initial attachments to my appearance, things felt better for a while. But the truth was, I needed to do more.

You see, that's what trips us up on the journey of self-exploration. We fix a problem and think that's it—but if we stop there, we miss the *real* lasting transformation. We end up just weeding out all the bad (which can then easily grow back) instead of breaking ground on an entirely new garden. Ultimately, that's how we end up believing that the absence of bad is the qualifier for good in our life. I had to recognize that it wasn't sobriety from substances that would save my life; *it was sobriety from my attachments and the old version of myself* that would save me. I literally had to detox from my old self in order to become the person I am today. And *that* is the sobriety that saved my life.

You may not be addicted to prescription pills, but I wasn't either for the first twenty-four years of my life. I was addicted to myself, to my hair, to praise from other people, to relationships, to my accomplishments, to pleasing people around me, and to my ability to top myself again and again. Eventually, I became addicted to remaining the person I was, the person I knew. I was in a committed relationship with my old self until my old self almost killed me, then only because I was forced did I go deeper inside and begin the journey of truly saving my life.

You may think your life doesn't need to be saved, but let

me tell you something from sheer experience. As a woman who almost died at the hands of substances *and* as a woman who also almost died on the inside at the hands of all the shiny objects to which I was deeply attached—the latter threatened my existence in a much greater way. Those things stole my life while I was still living.

By letting go of chapel singing I discovered I had to be open to the possibility of another version of myself, one that wasn't attached to anything on the outside or hiding behind any kind of mask. It was a journey of faith, it was believing without knowing what was on the other side. These attachments got really strong and sticky. And they held me back for a long time.

Sometimes, we think we have seen the problem and we've nipped it in the bud. That's what happened to me. But it could be that we haven't looked quite deeply enough yet. We haven't completely gotten it. Are you willing to go a little further? And to explore those inner layers where maybe you're still hanging on to some vestiges of what you want—or need—to change about your old self?

How a Good Thing Turns Bad

Pastor and author Timothy Keller popularized the idea that there are four deep motivations that we often and easily become addicted to, and they are: power, control, comfort, and approval. The fourth one on that list is the one I've wrestled with for my entire life. And third is the one that we all have to wrestle with daily in order to live a bigger life. Our desire for any of those four things can get so strong that it destroys us from the inside out. Our constant pursuit of them will drive us mad.

When I surrendered the microphone in chapel, I was surrendering my final attachment, my need for praise or approval from others. *But*—this is key—it wasn't that singing in church was a bad thing. On its face, that's generally believed to be a very positive use of one's time. Even things that outwardly appear to be selfless and positive can still become an unhealthy attachment and can block you from doing the deeper work. It is not the act itself that matters; it's all about the *meaning* we attach to it. Once I was able to do the work and let go of that need for validation, then singing in church or anywhere else was no longer an issue for me.

A perfectly healthy activity can become an unhealthy attachment if we are driven by an unhealthy motivation. If we are not comfortable in who we are and we are obsessively seeking power, control, comfort, or approval, then any good thing can turn bad.

The shiny objects in our lives can stunt our growth and keep us stuck living half a life, and for me, that meant a life that was defined by comments, compliments, and accolades from others. That's the same thing as handing over the reins of our lives to strangers. And these fronts we put on for the world? They can seem harmless, and even benevolent (like leading the church in song), but where we run into trouble is when we define ourselves by the front, not by who we truly are.

Seriously, look around at how common this is. When did we begin to stack all of these things in front of us in order to somehow prove our worth? Just look at Instagram: "This is me, the real me, world. Look! I'm nailing it in my career. I've read thirty books this year. I'm an amazing mom; my children have no screen time. I graduated top of my class. I wake up at 5 a.m., meal prep, meditate, and work out, all before 7 a.m." You know; all the things we want others to know about us so they can approve us accordingly. Why do we care so deeply about what others think of us that we lose ourselves under the weight of the shiny things in the process? It's like a kind of currency we spend on one another.

I remember when people would ask me the question "So, what do you do?" and I would always find a way to work my accomplishments into my answer. It was like I needed to lead with those things in order to feel confident that the other person even wanted to have a conversation with me.

What are your go-to's when you're introducing yourself to someone? In a five-minute conversation, what do you make sure people know about you? Do you feel the need to drop names and accolades? Do the words come tumbling out of your mouth before you even realize that you've been justifying your existence and worth to a total stranger? Your answers to those questions could reveal your own shiny objects.

Now, let's take this a step further. Who would you be if that thing that makes you feel special—your achievements, your talents, even your looks—was removed? Are you so defined by it that you're not even sure how to answer that question? If you had to strip it all off and walk around in the world as an average Joe or Jane, how would that feel? Would you want to wrap yourself in your shiny successes as quickly as possible, making sure everyone around you knew exactly what you're capable of? Would you immediately start grasping for the next shiny object you can hold out to others? It's scary to think about sometimes, but it's also so powerful. These things get a hold on us, and they do it silently, without us noticing. This is your opportunity to notice. And to check in with yourself from time to time to make sure you are not falling into that trap.

It took me a while before I was finally able to look in the mirror and know, *really* know, that I loved the person staring back at me, just as she was, without a single shiny thing or a full-blown cheering section. Now, I'm just hoping to save you a little time.

CHAPTER 5

Living in Legacy Mode

Staring up at the wooden beams of the cabin's bedroom, I listened to my breathing and tapped my hand on the blanket. Tap. Breath. Tap. Breath. Tap. My stomach churned and my jaw kept clenching. There would be no sleep, that was for sure. The thick Tennessee summer air weighed on my chest and the seconds ticked by as if stuck in syrup, slowed down to half speed. *Would the sun ever rise on this day?*

In just a few hours' time, I would be standing in a circle of people, comprised of my siblings, parents, grandparents, aunts, uncles, and cousins, sharing the most shameful and life-altering thing I'd ever done. No wonder I couldn't sleep.

As soon as the first tiny slivers of light danced through the windows and across the floor of the cabin, I took one last deep breath and forced my feet to the ground. I felt like the snake who was about to shed its skin for all to see, and I just wanted the whole thing to be over.

This day would be a part of my story for a long time; I could feel it. For fifteen years, the Ervin family had been gathering at various locations like this one, set deep in the woods, to take an intentional pause and talk about who we are in the world, both as a family and as individuals. It was like a family reunion, but with a specific purpose. We'd even had guest speakers come and talk to us about various topics that would help us make more informed life decisions. It was pretty awesome, really.

Some families believe that the wisdom and knowledge they want to impart to their children will just seep into them as if by osmosis. That simply living and thinking a certain way for the next generation to witness is enough. It may very well be, but my family wanted to be sure, so they took it a step further. Because in the opinion of the people who raised me, legacy is something even a child should consider. And that your legacy cannot, and should not, be left to chance. This was their way of getting us to think and talk about our legacy so that we could then go live with purpose. To my family, legacy extends beyond our one life—it can be the foundation for the next generation. It's our nonmonetary inheritance. Living fully is really for us; a legacy goes *beyond* us.

That particular year, however, it felt like all the fun and all the learning was going to be just out of my reach. Like I was suddenly separate, not a part of the experience as in times past. I was smack in the middle of treatment, but because of my progress, I had received a weekend pass and I felt like the prodigal daughter, returning and asking, hoping, and wondering if I would be welcomed back in.

I knew in a few short hours, we would be telling stories. And stories, well, we knew a lot about those in my family. Storytelling is how we impart wisdom not only gained but earned by the previous generations and how we remember where we came from. Even we, a family who knew one another so deeply, needed these stories to inform our future.

I thought about the story my grandmother had shared once about birthing a baby in the middle of a hurricane, and then walking out of the hospital, loading two other children and a Shetland pony named Flicka into a Volkswagen bug, and traveling alone from Louisiana to Kentucky. My grandma has grit, and it filled us with pride to know we had her blood running through our veins.

I thought about the stories my grandfather had shared over the years of all the many hats he's worn. Pig farmer, mobile home–business owner, grocery store clerk, used car salesman, pawnshop owner, he did it all. When one business didn't work out, he never let the grass grow under his feet for very long—he was on to the next thing. He was truly the original entrepreneur, long before switching careers was popular.

When he was a farmer and a terrible blight wiped out his entire livelihood, he refused to even consider bankruptcy, which the bank was urging him to do. He believed "credit is all a poor man's got." He refused to compromise his principles in order to take what he believed to be the easier route. All the big farmers in our hometown declared bankruptcy, but my grandpa declared something different. To an outsider (and even to my grandma), the situation was dire, and a lot of people would have gotten stuck, but he was determined. He owed hundreds of thousands of dollars to the bank, and back then, that amount would have been insurmountable to most people. But not to him. He kept moving. He started selling mobile homes, and within six months, he became the largest mobile home dealer in the state of Kentucky. Then, within one year, he paid the bank back, keeping his credit, his principles, his family, and his faith intact.

All the stories our family members had ever shared were like that—about overcoming adversity, finding a way when there seemed to be nothing but roadblocks. But no one had shared the kind of experience I was about to.

I was still working out the mess I had created. I hadn't already walked through the fire and come out on the other side victorious. I was still half wandering around in the dark and half scraping my way toward the light. I was about to stand alone as the one that had gone astray on this grand path my family had envisioned.

My Turn

I ventured out of my cabin, and when I showed up in the main gathering house, my family was all buzzing around drinking coffee and eating breakfast. The nervous energy was palpable when I walked into the room. My family knew I was in treatment for substance abuse, but this was the first time they'd seen me since I checked in. No one quite knew how to act around me. I smiled and tried to act normal, even though the whole situation felt like a movie about somebody else's life.

The day of exercises and discussions began, and my segment was right at the start. A beloved advisor who was like a member of our family turned to me carefully and said, "Mal, it's your turn." With each step I took toward the front of the room, I felt like a heavy weight was pushing down on my shoulders, and I was so wishing that I could be walking up there to share another one of my success stories, or a new goal, something, *any*thing but this. Tears burned in the corners of my eyes. I couldn't believe I'd let everyone down. It was as if a branch of our family tree was wilting and dying, and it was my fault.

I hadn't quite known what would happen when I got up there, but the truths came spilling out of me as if it was a confession. "This is what's been going on with me. I need to be honest with you because I've been keeping a secret for so long," I said. I then talked about how I had gone against our way of living. How I'd gotten myself into trouble with some prescriptions, and how I'd been so focused on achieving that I'd lost myself in my relentless pursuit of success. I explained to them what I learned about addiction. How it's a disease, and just like there was a specific recovery in getting well from other diseases, it was the same with this too. How I was in treatment, working through the layers, and finding my way back to me—the person they knew before. How I wasn't finished, and I had more work to do. I wasn't standing before them as a victor, but as someone still in the middle.

I looked out at the eyes of multiple generations staring back at me. They had quietly listened to every word I said. When I finished, there was just stillness. And then they started clapping. And *kept* clapping. I loved the sound of clapping; it was basically the soundtrack of my life. But never before had anyone clapped for me for something like this. Not for a performance I'd given, but for something I'd done . . . wrong.

"We're proud of you, Mal," one of my uncles said. *Proud* of me? I couldn't believe it. My family raised their hands and asked questions. They wanted to know how they could support me in my journey toward recovery, how they might have made things harder along the way, and whether it's difficult for a person like me to be around certain things. I answered every one of their questions standing there in the middle of the room, from the middle of my journey. And just like that, the prodigal daughter was welcomed with a loving embrace.

I had been so afraid that telling this new story of my life was somehow going to erase my old story. That it would mean everyone would forget all the good from my past and remember only this. But I had worried for nothing. This had somehow made me a leader in their eyes. When I stood up there and owned my flaws, my family saw the spark of something I had not yet seen. It takes strength to recognize when we've made a mistake or strayed from our values and beliefs, even more to admit it to ourselves, and much more to admit it to the people we love.

I knew that truth can be a dead bolt on our destiny if kept a secret. But it can unlock a new version of our life if we choose to speak it. Now I know that my new vision of my future was born in that moment, surrounded by my family. I had just created my living legacy.

NOT ONLY FOR AFTER WE'RE GONE

There are so many lessons in life that we learn from others that make sense when we hear them and sound good in our minds, but it's not really until we've gotten off track, been thrown a curveball, or walked through a fire that those lessons come to life for us. We had spent years talking about our family legacy and our individual legacies, and it had always been something I understood and believed in. But it wasn't until I had my own struggles that I really *got* it. That's when I put it into practice.

When we think about the word "legacy," we usually think about something we leave behind after we die. It's something that gets engraved on our tombstone. But what I learned from my family, and what I've seen with my own eyes, is that we can live our daily lives with our legacy in mind. The way we choose to live our days on this earth can be an inspiration to others in the present, not just after we're gone. By exchanging the belief that a legacy is something we leave behind for the truth that we are living it *right here and now*, we step into our ability to live fully.

Many times at our family meetings, we were asked by the speaker to share what we felt our individual legacies would be. We wrote letters to ourselves, decorated bourbon barrels, wrote mission statements. One weekend we called Legacy Weekend, we were to depict our legacy on a wooden circle to present to the group. I decorated mine with a forest of white trees and a path that cut through them. At the end of the path was a flame with light shining all around it. I wanted my legacy to be one of light, of spreading a message, of sharing my own journey through the forest that led to the brightest life.

As other family members shared their legacy statements, we were carving into our minds the things we wanted for our lives, and at the same time, accepting the responsibility of helping guide one another toward our goals. You see, we are a family that doesn't leave a member behind when they fall; we go after the lost sheep.

You Have a Choice in Your Legacy

I've seen a lot of people my age trying everything they can to separate themselves from their families, and of course I get that sometimes it's for the best. We can't choose the people we're born to, and there are a lot of families that don't have legacies they'd want to pass on to the next generation. But you do have a choice in what legacy you live out today, and that can fuel you to forge a new path. You have a lot of influence over the people in your life, and *you* are the first generation of a new legacy. You're the base of your family tree.

Sometimes people break away from their family because they want to prove themselves as independent individuals who don't need any help or assistance. But I feel I am able to be who I am while simultaneously leaning on the lessons of my family's hard-fought battles. I weave their lessons and experiences into my life today. I'm so grateful to have this rare group of people around me that come together like a team in a huddle before going out to play the game of life. I think about all of the valuable inspiration I've gained inside that huddle, and I want that information to be part of my legacy.

As I get further from my younger years, those days of soaking up lessons helped me create my own vision for the future. Visualization also plays a big role in how I frame my legacy. I visualize my sons talking to their friends when they get older. How will they describe me as their mother? I want my children to remember me paying attention to them, being a present parent, having fun with them. I want them to remember a household of joy but also one in which we take on life's challenges without burying our heads in the sand.

What do you want people to know you for? Not only after you're gone, but how would they describe you today? Do you want them to see you as fun loving and vibrant? Do you want them to seek you out, ask for your wisdom? Think about how people react when you walk into a room. You can tell a lot about the kind of life you lead by the way people act in your presence. Are they happy to be around you? Or are they guarded, not sure they can relax in your presence? You can also look around at others who have a strong living legacy and weave those attributes into your own way of living fully.

VALUES: THE CORE OF OUR LEGACY

In order to make living our legacy a daily action, I like to think of it as living in legacy mode. What does that look like? Well, the best place to start is with your specific set of values. Living each day in legacy mode means living each day in accordance with what you value the most.

It helps to list your values, and then rank them from most important to least. Maybe faith and spiritual practices are at the top of your list. Or perhaps it's family. Maybe expressing your creativity is of high importance to you. Or helping others. It might be seeking adventure that matters most. Or connecting with community. Seeking justice for those who can't do it alone. Building deep friendships. Creating security for yourself and your family. The list is endless. But the key is to know what you value the most so that you can always keep those things in your sight.

Next, ask yourself this: Do your daily behaviors align with your values? In other words, do you make decisions that reflect what is most important to you? If we say one of our top values in life is one thing but then all the hours in our day are spent doing something else, this will block us from living in legacy mode. Seeking that value alignment is the key that unlocks our ability to create a living legacy, one that we can feel good about now and after we're gone.

An inheritance of silver and gold will only get you so far. There is nothing more valuable than human capital. I have seen the power of a living legacy, one in which we offer a piece of ourselves. Our life will expire. Our legacy will live, both now and forever.

CHAPTER 6

Fine Is the New Rock Bottom

"I'm fine." Those two words have rolled off my tongue a time or two in the sweetest of Southern accents, served up with a side of a bold-faced lie. I've said this "sentiment" to the bank teller, the grocery store clerk, and even my parents literally seconds after hearing from a doctor that if I continued along this path, I'd die. In the face of death, *fine*? Really?

So, let's talk about fine, which is, in my opinion, the new version of rock bottom. You know . . . rock bottom—when the situation is so bad you *have* to make a change. Typically we think of rock bottom when a drug addict or alcoholic is in their darkest, lowest point; it means either they need to start climbing out of that hole or they are going to die. Here's what I want you to know—being "fine" is also a life-or-death decision—because fine is an emotional death—the death of a full life.

Perhaps you've been telling yourself that you're fine for so long that you absolutely, wholeheartedly, without a shadow of a doubt believe that it's true and that it is enough for you.

Maybe you're thinking "I can skip this chapter because my life really *is* fine. I have no complaints. Life is all right, I guess. Steady. Okay, for the most part. I mean, at least nothing is really *wrong*." If that's what you're thinking and how you're feeling, I've got a great big red flag in my hand, and I'm waving it for you—hard. Why? Well, the absence of bad is not the qualifier for good.

I understand the allure of "fine" because it's predictable and safe, and it doesn't leave anything to chance. We get into our comfortable routines, and we convince ourselves that it's all good. Why bother with door number two when door number one is familiar? There might be adversity lurking behind door number two. There might be uncomfortable truths or challenges we don't believe we have the strength to face. It might require relentless effort, tough conversations, or even actual, real-life, in-your-face pain.

Well, "fine" may be the opposite of uncomfortable, but it is also the opposite of growth. Comfortable and easy sound good, but not when it means sacrificing creativity, passion, drive, experiences, enthusiasm, and ultimately, the life we really want. The truth is, living fine means risking the loss of living fully. We simply can't have it both ways. I know, because I've tried.

It's really easy to make a life transition when there's a red flag waving front and center, like a drug addiction, an affair, a child with a serious behavior issue, an eating disorder, depression, the list goes on. These things prompt you or your people to band together and figure out a path forward. Yes, you have to do the work once you get the nudge, but that first step is often taken with the help of someone else.

When you don't *have* to make the change, when things might even seem okay (but they really aren't), that's when it's the hardest to do so. Hard, but not impossible. Not for you.

So, if you are floating through life right now feeling like pretty good is good enough, well, you'd better get ready because you are about to experience a "fine" intervention. You get one shot here, just one life, and I don't want you spending it on the sidelines. I want to help you get fully into your life and play it with all your heart.

What's Your Flavor of Fine?

I've come to realize "fine" comes in a variety of flavors, and through the years I got well acquainted with my flavors of fine, and even gave them names: **smoky, smothered, complacent, and distracted.** They might sound like specials on a Waffle House menu, but I promise you they were nowhere near as delicious.

1. You know **smoky,** I'm sure. It's all about smoke and mirrors. We put on a happy face for the world, just keep smiling, but underneath, we are hurting, suffering in the silence that feels unrelenting. Show the best, hide the rest. We know we've got issues, but we don't have a clue how to face them. Just like a magician hiding the secrets of his magic, we use illusions to cover our pain and appear perfectly put together to anyone on the outside.

2. Then there is **smothered,** which is just sucking all the life out of you. It's that little voice in your head asking "Is this all there is?" "Does everybody feel this way?" "Is this how we are all getting through life?" We throw our shoulders back and in our most convincing, confident whisper, tell ourselves we're fine. Whew. That little voice vanished. You did it. You feel good . . . for a moment. But there is still a small voice deep down, because we can never completely silence it.

3. **Complacent** might be the easiest flavor of fine to slide into. We believe that this is just the way our life is, we have no control over it, so why bother even trying to make a change? We figure we were born into this life, and we're resolved to blindly accept it for what it is. Relinquishing the controls of our life, we slip silently into autopilot.

4. The most reliable flavor of fine, and the one we can count on every time, is **distracted.** We can make ourselves so busy that we never bother to check in with ourselves at all, so we literally have no idea how we're really feeling inside. We're all about taking care of anyone and everyone else, except us. Or we're just so busy all the time that we never pause long enough to think about our lives. Or maybe we like to be so busy that we can't stop and give ourselves even a moment to think how *not* okay we are. The distractions are actually diversions; they can divert us from our true feelings and eventually our true path.

One trait all these categories of fine have in common is that they resemble a daytime slumber, a twilight state of being that has you coasting along, totally oblivious to the incredible life you *could* be living, a life beyond the horizon you've created for yourself. It's "beyond" because you've stopped dreaming, you've stopped stretching, reaching, and pushing yourself. You've settled. And settling means you are wasting your life, or at least a pretty amazing version of it.

The Fine Lie

When I was in treatment, I finally came to terms with my new title of "addict who needed professional help," and I was able to do some decent work in the first month. At the end of the first thirty days, I knew my therapist would reassess my situation to see if I could leave or if I needed further assistance to help me transition back into my life with lesser odds of relapse. I thought that once I put all my numbing agents into a little box, I was perfectly fine and fixed underneath and could then re-emerge back into society and write a book. Ha!

My parents came for my assessment, and I waited for them in my therapist's office. When they walked in I smiled, beaming with a fresh face and newfound pride, ready to show the world what a new me looked like. A more relatable version of myself with a clear head of ideas and new goals. I couldn't wait for them to see it too.

I thought I had just taken a quick sabbatical to save my life, and I was ready to go about my typical day-to-day again and even help other people eventually. I thought I'd be going home. Once again, I was deluding myself. The truth was, I was living a different version of rock bottom.

I received a punch to the gut when my therapist, who I already had a problem with because she was the first to uncover a lot of my deeper issues I had to face, said, "We're recommending extended stay for you. Another three months at least. We feel we haven't addressed the why of it all. We haven't explored how you got here, and that's essential for true recovery."

I instantly replied, "Um, *what*? But I'm good now! I'm literally completely better now, I'm perfectly fine." I even said the word there. I fought and battled and cried and shut down. I looked at my dad—usually the easiest one to get on my side and help enable me—but to no avail. Still, I didn't give up. I just kept fighting and explaining, trying mightily to convince everyone to let me go home and to allow me to exist at that level. It was enough for me to finally feel okay; that's all I wanted. I had no desire to go deeper because fine felt so much better than bad. But no matter what I said, they saw more for my life. And deep down I knew they were right.

So I stayed.

And I did the most important work of my life. I got to the core of my issues, released my attachments, and emerged nearly *four* months later with the reins of my life back in my hands. That's when I realized the biggest shifts in our life happen not only when we take back the reins, but when we realize what drove us to this behavior in the first place.

When you evaluate your life, you might start to come to grips with the fact that even though you thought you were just fine, this is not the version of your life that you want. It might have snuck up on you, but now that you're putting some focus into it, you're seeing the truth.

When we spend our lives telling that fine lie, and we're really checked out and numbed out, we *miss out*. We miss out on what life really has for us. We miss living life guided by our true desires and values. When we're fine with being fine, we miss out on transforming into the version of the person for which we want to be remembered. I don't want you to miss that. I can't let you miss that.

An Invitation to a Fuller Life

When I was Miss Kentucky, I did a lot of speaking at schools. Sometimes I spoke at up to seven schools on any given day. I think most people don't realize the job of a pageant winner is a real, full-time, paying job where you do a *lot* of work. I traveled the entire state wearing a crown and a sash and entering into the sacred spaces of the most impressionable people, our youth. I must have given speeches to three hundred or more schools that year.

Often, I would speak to children in impoverished parts of the state. Like a lot of states in our nation, Kentucky has certain vulnerable areas that I never realized existed. I'll never forget the things I experienced when I traveled to those regions, or the way it opened my eyes and changed me. The schools hold a special place in my heart, and those kids are some of the reasons I share my story and strive to help people change their lives to this day. One of the messages I shared at every school was that we, all of us, can choose to do whatever we want with our lives.

Speaking to a crowd of kids packed into a gymnasium, I'd say, "You can choose the life you want." I can still remember the looks on some of their faces—often of visible shock, as if no one had ever told them that before. If I could go back now, I would say something a bit different. I would add that, yes, it requires constant hard work, and unfortunately it takes a lot more for some to even get up to the starting line, but choosing a fuller life is worth it in the end.

I used to get into my car sometimes and cry when I left those schools, wondering why they had to climb out of a well before they could even get to the business of living fully. I still don't know the answer to that. But I do know this. This is the life we were given and we can choose to let the unfair disadvantages determine our future, or we can fight to overcome what we can until the world can make up for the difference. And I hope the world will make up that difference soon. I, for one, think we should never stop fighting to live a better way.

At one school where I spoke, the administrators accidentally included a photocopy of my business card with my cell phone number on the signed photo that went home with all the students. I can still remember the first call, when I picked up the phone and a little voice on the other end said, "Miss Kentucky? I have a question. If my mom says I can't be a marine biologist because we don't live near the ocean, do you really think I still could? If I worked really, really hard?"

One by one, dozens of children called for guidance on how they could overcome their circumstances. They already wanted more for their lives. Although it was a mistake that my number was given to hundreds of elementary school students, it was not a mistake to learn how, even at that young age, we all have a deep hunger to be better than fine. Those kids kept me on my toes for a couple of weeks, but it reminded me that the desire to dream bigger starts when we're young, but then the desire for comfort over everything creeps in as we get older.

I want to tell you—in case no one's told you before—the same thing I told those students: *a fuller life is available to you.* That life may look different from your parents' and friends' lives, from your coworkers' or in-laws'. Heck, it might even look different from your entire generation. No matter where you're starting from, you have the invitation. We all will have different work to do on our way to that version of life, but we all have the same invitation.

What does that life look like? Envision the life you want, down to the specifics. Give yourself permission to dream big. Picture the job, the home, the people in it, the way you feel in it. How do the details of that elevated version of life compare to your current life? What is different, and what is the same? Is there a huge gap that makes it glaringly obvious that you have been coasting and living a life that is just fine? I believe you have the answers inside you. And some of those answers will be unearthed by looking at what you like or dislike about how you are living life in the here and now.

This is the most important invitation you have ever received.

So why don't we take the invitation?

Because everything's fine.

When we've settled for fine, it's hard for us to even imagine what fuller would look like. But I hope now you realize that won't cut it any longer. Even if it's hard overcoming the allure of fine, it can lead you to unimaginable places. Fine may be the new rock bottom, but rock bottom is the perfect foundation on which to build your incredible new life.

PART II
Staying Awake

CHAPTER 7

Don't Let Your Blessings Become Your Burdens

My dad is a genius. He's the type of genius that can install fiber-optic networks across the United States but would have a tough time on a third-grade spelling test. He wears camouflage in meetings with HBO executives and runs a *very* successful company out of a corporate office in the middle of a cornfield in Kentucky because he wanted to raise a family in the small town where he grew up. If you've ever listened to my podcast, you know that my dad's advice is simple and sound. He has it all figured out.

Every time he writes me a card, it has the same message in it. It's his ultimate life lesson he's given to me at church retreats, written in graduation cards, and spoken of at any sort of event or milestone where people contribute life advice. Of all the different types of advice he offers people, it's funny that he gives me this same piece over and over.

Sometimes, when I've received a bunch of cards, say on my birthday, I always save his until last, and once I've gone through all the notes everyone else has written me, I'll think, okay, here it comes: my dad's letter is going to tell me some profound secret to life. His key to life. I'll start to read the note, and once it dawns on me that he's talking about balance for the one millionth time, I'll be like, *Dad, why are you telling me this again? You said the same thing last time!* But I think it's because I'm the person who really *needs* this advice over and over. Maybe we all are.

"Balance," he writes (sometimes he spells it "balence," even when he types it, and I swear he purposely rejects the spellcheck and spells it his own way), "is one of the most important things in life." Then he writes out a list of words like "work," "family," "faith," "passions." "At times, you will get out of balance and this will bring on hardships. When you lose your balance, you lose yourself. So, you have to find that balance again."

Even when I was a little kid, he wrote about all those life stages, some of which didn't apply to me yet. For instance, as a kid, "family" would equate to balancing my time between my siblings, parents, and grandparents. I didn't have a job yet, so it was interesting that my dad included the work category anyway. It was like he was delivering a grown-up message to a child. I know there are countless instances when we need kid messages as grown-ups. Advice like be kind to other people, take a nap, take a time-out, wash your hands. Well, I think my dad knew that by sharing this grown-up advice with me as a child, he was planting a seed, one that would sprout and grow and take on a life of its own as I got older.

I think this message about balance is one of the simplest lessons I've been taught, but it's as complex to navigate as the stars in the sky. The concept is easy. It's the practice that's hard. That's why I need so many reminders about it.

Why Imbalance Is the Enemy

I'm an extreme person. I go all in on things. Balance seems average and boring and a little too practical and buttoned-up for me. But let me tell you why my dad's advice became a cornerstone for me and why mastering balance can be the North Star in our quest for a meaningful life.

We've all barely made it through times when our lives were chaotic. It's usually a season like raising young children, making it through college, young adulthood, starting a new business, or moving on from a relationship we've been in for so long. Sometimes seasons require us to be plopped down on one side of the seesaw with the other end soaring skyward. But these imbalances usually correct themselves as our circumstances change—we graduate, the kids get older, we get more focused on our career. These imbalances are not the ones that threaten our fulfillment.

The ones that endanger living a full life are the smaller ones we battle day to day. These imbalances, if left unchecked, can wreck our families, our relationships, our joy, and our entire lives. Of all the times my dad reminded me about balance through the years, I didn't realize it was the daily balancing acts that mattered the most. It was not until recently that it hit me right between the eyes and changed my life forever. Here's how it happened.

It was the summer of 2019, I had been posttreatment for five years, and I'd reunited with my boyfriend (now husband) Kyle. The first time we dated we'd talked about marriage, but he was right when he made the hard decision that we should break up. I was not well and in turn our relationship couldn't be either. But it seems our love transcended all that I went through in treatment, because once we reconnected, we knew what we suspected all along—that we were meant to be together. We got married and had our first son and I got pregnant with our second baby—all within two years.

Simultaneously, I'd been building my business and I'd created the Living Fully brand, which was gaining lots of traction. It was around this time that I also started a podcast called *Living Fully with Mallory Ervin*. I'd been having amazing, open-ended conversations with my friends and heroes about what it meant to live life to the fullest—Gabby Bernstein, Bob Goff, Jeremy Camp, Jen Hatmaker, Katherine Schwarzenegger, Vivica Fox, and many others. It just so happened that this was the very first episode I recorded and it was with a dear friend of mine, author Jessica Turner.

Just to set the stage a bit for you, the recording was to take place in my home, which was spotless. It always was then. I had all the pillows karate-chopped and every one of my son's toys and snacks organized in a perfect rainbow in some closet out of sight. I had a diffuser going, a candle burning, and a huge bouquet of fresh flowers sitting on the counter. That's just how I rolled. Because that was important to me.

Jessica and I were sitting at my dining room table. Before I even asked the first question—

Jessica: "Your house is so clean!"

Me: "Oh, my housecleaners just left." (That was true but they had only done about 50 percent of it. I had obsessed over the rest and made my son and husband play upstairs in the hours leading up to it so it didn't get messed up again.)

Jessica: "Mine is always a mess."

No way, I thought. *Who is she kidding? It seems like she's always got it so together. No way her house is a mess.*

Jessica (noticing my pause): "Because I'd rather be spending time with my kids than keeping the house clean."

We laughed a little but then . . .

Me: "Wait, what?"
Jessica: "Yeah, have you ever heard of how everything we juggle is either a glass ball or a rubber ball?"

She went on to explain a brilliant juggling analogy that originally came from former Coca-Cola CEO Brian Dyson, who delivered a commencement speech at Georgia Tech in the nineties. He said that in life, you're juggling glass balls, which are the most important things, and rubber balls, which aren't as important. If you drop the rubber balls, they'll do what you might expect a rubber ball to do—bounce back. But if you drop the glass balls, they won't bounce. They'll get cracked, or even shatter. The idea is to strive for balance and to focus your attention on the important things so that you don't drop the glass balls.* The glass balls are the parts of your life which you value most deeply. The rubber balls are the things that don't matter as much in the grand scheme of life.

That hit me real hard. What I realized was that I'd been mislabeling the balls. I was not treating the glass balls in my life as glass. I was mistaking them for rubber.

Our families, spouses, jobs, spiritual lives, these are the glass balls. If we continue to carelessly let them fall out of the juggling rotation while keeping our focus on the rubber balls, they go crashing to the ground and get cracked. Another drop. Another one. A final one, well, they shatter. So, we must be careful to keep our attention and care on the glass balls, and not drop them too many times. Because they will break forever.

The rubber balls, they're the things that can be dropped over and over and they won't break. The things that don't matter as much—our houses, our laundry, our schedules, our

* Brian Dyson, "Coca-Cola CEO's Secret Formula for Success: Vision, Confidence, and Luck" (commencement speech, printed in *The Georgia Tech Whistle*, Volume 17, Number 27, Sept 30, 1991).

manicures—they can fall to the ground and bounce right back. They don't shatter. They'll always be okay.

Jessica and I went on to have a long conversation about how the problem starts when we mistake the glass balls for rubber balls. Our families? If we keep flitting around our homes obsessively cleaning up instead of sitting down with our people, that's a glass ball dropped. If we stop calling our parents or grandparents because we're too busy with a million things or because we watch our show on Sunday night, that's a glass ball dropped. If we stop communicating with our spouses and asking what we need from each other because we're scrolling on social media, or too tied up with work, that's a glass ball dropped. Drop those glass balls too many times and eventually, they will shatter. And here's the thing, you can't go to the store and buy new ones. So we must keep our eyes and attention on the glass balls that matter.

Everyday Balance

That analogy changed a lot of how I look at balance. As I've learned to live more presently, not all mixed up in my old titles or super concerned with future ones, I realize that choosing balance is how we can change our lives long term as well as the lives of the people around us. But it's that everyday balance that counts.

For me, nighttime hours are especially hard for keeping a good balance. It's when I spend time creating content for social media. From what I'm picking out of the garden and making for dinner, to the outfits the kids are in, to what they're doing with Kyle in the backyard—there's a lot going on. Sometimes I feel like I'm sitting in the middle of the ball pit at Chuck E. Cheese, cradling a little glass ball as thousands of rubber ones are flying all around me.

But the key for me is to remember that I pull content

from the life I've created—not the other way around. That's how I stay balanced when my profession and my life are so closely entwined. My time, energy, and focus are on creating the *life*, not creating the content. And when I find myself focusing too much on things like, *Oh, I need to order ten pairs of new kids' pajamas to feature, and I've got to film three videos on dinner ideas and share an updated nighttime skin-care routine*, I simply step back and remind myself: all I need to do is show what's actually going on in my life. I create the life. That's the content for social media.

Stay with me here, because even if you're not an influencer, you have an audience. We all have audiences. We all think about who's watching us, who's looking at how we live our lives. Our boss, our friends, the people in the drop-off line at school. So, the question you have to ask yourself when you're putting on the outfit, or planning the beach vacation, or going to a trendy hot spot—are you planning the *pictures* or planning your *life*? Your life is the glass ball, the pictures are the rubber ball. If you can look back on a weekend and know that you actually connected with your loved ones, that's what balance feels like. Even if you missed the opportunity for a cute photo, you can know that you prioritized what mattered most.

There are always going to be those rubber balls tempting us to focus on them. We have to fight to keep our eye on what's important and not get lost in everything else.

Keeping Everyday Balance

Easier said than done, right? Here's what helped me: remembering that balance is not something you strive for and achieve once; it's something you practice every day. It requires some self-awareness in the moment. It's choices we can make daily, to prioritize the glass balls over the rubber ones.

- It's choosing to leave the dirty dishes in the sink and sit down with the kids after dinner to play.

- It's going on the midweek date night instead of working late.

- It's turning off your devices and having a night unplugged with your family.

- It's having a heart-to-heart conversation with your partner, child, family member, or close friend, instead of just texting them.

- It's putting off your errands for a little while so you can call a friend or family member and ask—*really* ask—how they're doing.

- It's a gut check that asks, *Am I feeling out of balance today? Is there something I can spend more time on in order to get it back?* These gut checks can reveal a lot about what we've been prioritizing.

Keeping Balanced During the Big Things

Finding and maintaining balance on the day-to-day can be challenging enough, but it's especially tough to keep it when we're in the midst of preparing for those big life moments that don't come along too often. For instance, when we're planning a wedding or a birthday party or any other event that marks a milestone in our lives, we have to be vigilant to stay balanced.

I'd sung at over a hundred weddings by the time I went to college, and I was always amazed at what aspects brides would focus on. They'd spend months, even years, planning their wedding day down to the tiniest details of the garter, or the hair clip, or the correct shade of eggshell the napkins should be. Imagine if they'd spent even some of that time focused on learning how to have a great marriage, instead of just an epic wedding day for five hours!

How we define balance changes over time too. As a young person, the stakes didn't feel as high to me. But once I had more skin in the game, a family, kids, work, and so on, I suddenly felt the weight and magnitude of balancing those things that matter *big time* and those things that don't matter as much in the day-to-day. That's what it took for me to finally grasp this concept and start using it in my daily life. The stakes became too high to not get this right.

BLESSING OR BURDEN: THE ROOT OF IMBALANCE

I've thought a lot about how we get imbalanced, and why we often neglect things that we asked for in the first place. I think it's because we let our blessings—things that we yearned for, prayed for, worked for, fought for, and *won*—become our burdens.

Do you often say you want to improve your health, but you don't commit any time in your schedule to eating healthy foods or exercising? Do you live in your athleisure clothes but spend way more time in the leisure than the ath? Maintaining our physical health is what allows us to be around for those we love, and to feel good enough to enjoy our lives. Good health is a blessing, but we often view maintaining it as a burden.

Or maybe it's your work. Are you in your dream career? With a full-blown team, an office, and a packed calendar? But you're so stressed and so busy you can't even see straight? I'm bad about this one. I spin out of control, making a hundred lists for a hundred people doing a hundred things at a hundred miles per hour—and my Lord, this is what I asked for in the first place! What I dreamed of in the first place!

Why the heck do we mislabel our dreams as nightmares sometimes? *We got the things we wanted, but we constantly have to work to want the things we got.* That's the key to seeing them through the blessing lens, not the burden one. Then once we see them clearly again we can begin juggling them again in the right rotation.

Part of the way to keep our blessings from becoming our burdens is to zoom out to a whole-life view and really look at the things we spent so much time wishing for. Then we can reframe just enough to see them clearly again. The other part is recognizing that blessings take work. And that's okay.

Are you feeling out of balance? Think about your blessings and ask yourself if you've allowed them to become burdens in your mind. Very often, that simple, intentional awareness is enough to help you put them back into their correct category. Keeping them there is something you can now choose to do on a daily basis.

So, my dad was right in all of those letters he wrote me over the years. Balance *is* one of the most important things to master in our lives. And I figured out why he reminded me of this again and again; it's because balance is never really mastered on a grand scale in our lives. It is mastered in the details. In the daily choices. Choosing to correctly label and then fiercely protect the things we value most is how we do it. And that's exactly what I've watched him do for all these years. Thanks, Dad.

CHAPTER 8

Endangered Species

In the middle of writing this book, my family and I took a quick trip to Kentucky. There had been a constant need for entertainment, especially with two baby boys under the age of two. Our usual vacation spot was closed due to the coronavirus pandemic, so we opted to spend a weekend at the family farm where I grew up.

It was two weeks before the first half of this book was due to my editor, and I was in the fine-tuning phase of a couple of chapters. I needed to be working on them but I also needed a reprieve and a dose of inspiration. More than that, though, I felt a magnetic pull to be in the place where I grew up. I think this chapter was tugging at me, asking to be written.

The way I grew up was a rarity. I was raised on a huge farm along with all twenty-three of my first cousins (on my dad's side), with me being the oldest. I had an idyllic childhood there. The kind they make TV series and movies about. One they write books about. Both of my grandparents are still alive and they still live in the center of the farm, and my dad's siblings have homes in every direction around the property. We jokingly call it a compound—but all joking aside, it kind of *is* a compound.

My cousins were like my siblings, and then my best friends as I grew older. We all roamed back and forth between one another's houses. We had acres of gardens, pumpkin patches, and a sleigh we rode in for the Christmas parade downtown. (I am pretty sure one of my uncles was Santa, but to us, that was the real Mr. Claus riding with us.) We caught fish, snakes, and wild cats with our bare hands, and we helped birth farm animals. We learned to build things and sell things and do things, all under the watchful one good eye of my grandpa. (A case of chicken pox stole the vision out of his other eye at a young age.)

My grandpa—PaPa Bud—is as close to an ideal person as I've ever known. Maybe you know someone like him—the type of person you smile at the thought of seeing. Someone who is quick to laugh. They listen with their ears and their heart, and they never talk just to talk. When they do speak, it's exactly what you needed to hear. This person truly embodies what it means to live fully. It's like they made a wedding vow to life and kept it. *I'll take you, life, for richer or poorer, in sickness and in health, I'll honor you all of my days*. They honor life. They never waste it.

My papa has endured a lot of pain in his life. He was literally born of pain, a thirteen-pound baby to a fourteen-year-old girl. She was already married, but still just a child. Times were different then. When my papa was just twelve years old, he watched his father die as he ran into their burning home to save their family's guns and the house collapsed around him. His sister was hit by a car after pushing him off the tandem bike they were riding, saving his life and sacrificing hers. When I ask him how he made it through hard times like those, he always says, "We never had any hard times."

Any one of these things would practically end most of us.

Or me, at least. But these things made Bud Ervin the man who breathed life into more than sixty human beings, and he continues to breathe life into us even now. All that pain is what formed the beauty in him, and he passed down that beauty to his entire family. A spirit of love, forged in the fire of pain. He simply didn't see it as something painful he had to endure; it was just life.

As I spent time with my grandpa and my grandma Marylyn that weekend, I was reminded of all their strengths, and it made me wonder: Why am I so fearful of adversity when it seems that everyone I admire was literally built from it? Not in a "yeah, I made it through that" kind of way but in an "I was *made* through that" kind of way. What I've learned from my grandparents is that how we choose to deal with pain not only reveals our true character, but it strengthens it. I know I can look back on my own tribulations and see how they refined me. How those challenges pushed me to change when I would never have done it on my own.

Forged Through Fire

My grandpa, even at eighty-five years old, still works long hours in the hot sun, gardening, canning vegetables, and doing anything and everything for his family. Just like he always has. He never stops, not even as a chronic lung disease has made it harder for him to breathe. He'll cough and cough, and then smile and shake his head saying, "Shoo-wee!"

"What's wrong, PaPa? Can they give you something for it? What do you think it is?"

"Father Time, Mally," he'll say. I always hate when he talks about Father Time.

On that particular trip, his declining health seemed more obvious than in times past. I felt this bottomless ache. An ache for him not to feel pain. An ache of the pain we'll feel when we lose him. And then an ache to avoid the pain I felt that day. (I think that last one is a "my generation" thing—it seems we'll do anything to avoid pain.) I was so glad we were riding four-wheelers all weekend because the wind dried my tears before I'd get to him.

These days, we spend so much time avoiding pain, which is unfortunate because pain is the ingredient that can make the best among us. It is what shapes our legacy, even as we walk on this earth. I'm not speaking for everyone of my generation, of course, but I do see a common thread of pain avoidance that I find alarming. By avoiding pain, aren't we also hindering our ability to become a better version of ourselves as a trade-off for a more comfortable life?

The Good Ole Days Are Today

The more I talked to my grandparents that weekend, the more I realized they're like an endangered species. And in the same way we begin to mourn the loss of an animal species before it disappears into extinction, I was feeling that heavy sadness while my grandparents still lived and breathed.

Why do we do that? Why do we mourn, fear, ache over something or someone that's still here, right in front of us? It can hurt so deeply, as if they are already gone. But the ache was dulled when I remembered the good ole days don't have to just live in the past—they're happening right now. That truth washed over me, and I smiled as I watched my papa playing with my younger son. Treasuring the moment, not dreading the moment's end.

When I was a little girl, my grandparents drove me two and a half hours to Nashville every Wednesday after school for my voice lessons. In the car, we would talk and I would sing country songs for them, we would laugh, and I would ask them questions. I'd have my one-hour lesson, we'd eat dinner and then make the trip back home. When I was a child, it was always so easy to take them all in without worrying about when they weren't going to be here anymore. There was no pressure attached to our time together, no impending expiration date. Now that I'm older, I'm determined to get back to that mentality.

Our last night in Kentucky, we rode the four-wheelers across the field to their house to find my grandparents and my parents and uncles sitting on the back porch talking about birds and great-grandkids. I looked at my babies and then at theirs. Theirs all turned out to be people mostly similar to them, with so much of their strength, resilience, and love for family running through their veins. I wanted to ask my grandparents, "How did you raise your kids to be like that?" Like I've asked them so many times about all kinds of things, from how to pickle something or how to grow a tomato like theirs but in my raised bed in the city, or how to buy land or heal a cut some natural way. I wish they could give me a simple answer first, of how to be like them and second, how to raise a baby to be like them.

Honoring a Life Well Lived

That night in bed, I thought a lot about what it is that makes my grandparents so special. I know many people feel this way about their grandparents. We name our children after them, we share their family recipes that they perfected. We look up to what they've accomplished in amazement, the obstacles they had to overcome to get that far in life.

I've been told so many beautiful stories about Kyle's grandfather who came over from Italy with nothing but a passion for making shoes, and who lived a vibrant life a lot like my papa's. I believe the greatest way to honor them is to live our lives well, to see their wisdom and apply it, to never take our lives for granted, and to not let our fear of adversity overcome our ability to live fully. God knows they wouldn't have let that get in their way.

I've seen myself steering away from things that might bring pain, "cancellation," or major life shifts that are difficult. I've been through them before, but even the thought of enduring them again just makes me feel too tired. Too scared. You likely know what I'm talking about. But also, you can probably look back on your life and pinpoint an instance when you've made it through something you would rather have avoided, but now you can see that it made you a different person. And you are, in specific and unique ways, better because of it. What if every time we notice ourselves avoiding things that could bring us pain, we just accessed those memories as a reminder that on the other side of pain is always a fuller existence? What if we lived unafraid again? Or . . . better yet, more afraid of losing out on a life than of experiencing pain within it? I think that shift would bring us closer to living as they did. It's one way I can honor my grandparents with my life.

When I was in treatment, we did an exercise where we made a poster about the best person we knew, specifically someone who's had a big influence on our lives. I did mine on my papa. I wrote his qualities around a bubble with his name, and then I read each of them aloud to the group while weaving in several incredible stories illustrating what kind of person he is.

No one in the group said anything while I was speaking, and when I was done, I looked up and they were all staring right at me. I noticed a few of them were even crying. "That's you," someone said. "The way you just described your grandpa is how we describe *you*."

I couldn't take it in. I saw it but didn't see it at the same time. I couldn't accept the greatest words anyone ever said to me.

Looking back, I can see how, in that specific freeze-frame of my life, I was probably the closest I've ever gotten to really being like him. During my time in treatment, I had let go of all the bad stuff and all the clutter that just crowded out the good. I was the bare-bones version of myself for the first time since I was a little girl.

I think it was the purest version of living fully that I had experienced. My mindset had begun to shift and I was realizing that I liked that way of thinking and living so much better. But it wasn't until my peers reflected that truth to me that I realized I had never really gotten that far from who I am. I had only been blinded to it by my addiction and attachments, but with that all gone, it was much easier to see.

Have you ever had a moment where you realized who you are at your core? Maybe it was when someone else pointed it out to you, or when you saw a flash of yourself within the attributes of someone you admire. Those moments can serve as powerful reminders of the good you hold inside.

The Flow of Wisdom

I've come to believe there is a river of pure wisdom flowing through all of us. Our job is to acknowledge it, tap into it, and try not to block it. The people who have walked before us know what makes a full life because they've been through difficult times, they've survived loss. We can reap the benefits of their hard-earned wisdom and also honor them by infusing those lessons into our everyday living.

I've seen my grandpa loan money to people knowing he wouldn't get it back. He's never held a grudge against anyone in his life. He gives people chances again and again, and he forgives instantly. These are just some of the things I see and admire in him. I want so much to stay in that flow of wisdom, rather than just watch from the river's banks.

I know we are able to find it within ourselves. I've seen it. When we give things to people when the world isn't watching, or we take children into our homes. We pray for people without telling them, we give anonymously, both money and possessions. We put in longer, harder hours for the ones and the things we love. We take up for people when we know it will lead to our own harm. We all have that good stuff within us. But how can we be more like that *all* the time? And how do we tap into it when we've been dealt a tough hand? My grandpa always said, "You've got to play the hands that you're dealt." And that's exactly what he's always done, without complaint and without ever compromising who he is. I want to do that too.

Every so often when I'm talking to my grandparents about how they've lived, and pondering the future, I start to feel fear rising. Will Kyle and I even be able to raise good children with resilience, morals and kindness, and love for their families the way they did? Is that even possible in today's world? Maybe you've asked yourself some version of the same question.

Before we had to head home that weekend, I asked my grandparents what they thought about raising kids today. Things are so different now than back then. Staring out at the martin birdhouses he built so many years ago, my papa said, "I don't know, Mal. Once you let one cow out the gate, it's hard to keep the whole herd from getting out. And once they're all out, it's hard to get them back in."

He's right; it seems we as a society have moved away from some of those morals—the cows in his analogy—from resilience and from love. These "cows" have been slowly getting out of the gate the past few decades, and the world has gotten harsher for it. I think it's gotten more judgmental, and more divided too.

But the thing I've been wondering is—has the whole herd gotten out? Have we drifted too far from the values of our elders? Is it too late? I don't think so. Not yet, at least. If we lean on the wisdom of our very own human endangered species before they're gone, then we can help it live on. They may be endangered, but their wisdom does not need to be. We can raise the next generation not to fear adversity, but to face it head-on. We can choose resilience over reluctance because we've seen the types of people we can become when we walk through the fire. And we can choose to prioritize love and kindness even when no one's looking.

Will we become those people? I'm sure as heck trying to.

CHAPTER 9

Keeping the Faith

"Um, Father? It's Mallory Ervin, from your old church, um, in Morganfield," I said.

"Yes, hello, Mallory," he replied.

"Um, hi. How are you?" Without waiting for a reply, I blurted out, "I'm sorry to bother you. I just had a quick question about something." I skipped right over the "how are you" part, quickly feeling like I couldn't ask a priest how he was. I don't know why we put up these blocks about people in places of spiritual authority. Like they're the bouncers for heaven or something.

"Well, I love lighting candles when I say prayers." I continued, "Some for me, but I also pray a lot for other people." Again, trying to make my case and gain his spiritual approval. "I go to church a lot in Nashville, but sometimes I can't get there, or it's locked, or it's, like, nighttime and dark. . . ." Ugh—a churchy Valley girl. "So, I was just wondering, do you think it would be okay, maybe, if I had one of those candle stations in my house? My mom told me I had to ask you before she bought me one for Christmas, but I really want one, I have for years, and I feel like I could pray a lot more, and I would just feel way holier if I could . . ."

He solemnly interrupted my one-sided sermon. "That's fine, Mallory."

"Oh, really? Awesome! So, is there like a certain thing I need to do when it comes into my home or a special blessing I need on it to make it okay?" Holy word vomit.

"No, it's perfectly fine."

"Okay, thanks, Father. I'll say a prayer for you on it." Oh my Lord, did I for real just tell the priest I would pray for him? Yes. And I did.

On Christmas morning, I opened my last present, half-pouting that none of the packages under the tree for me had been a candle station (how un-Christlike of me). It was a single blue glass candle holder with a votive in it—a clue to the whole set that was hidden just around the corner. I looked up at my mom and yelled, "You found one? Oh my gosh, I get one? Where did you find it?"

She said, "Well, Father called me after you spoke with him and it just so happened that they were remodeling the church and they were getting rid of two, so he gave you this one."

Gently holding the votive in my hands, I cried inside. My holy golden ticket.

Now, for over ten years, I've been lighting candles at that station. I've sobbed through tears of heartbreak, the crippling paralysis of indecision, the loss of something I thought I couldn't live without, as well as in pure overflowing giddiness and thanksgiving, and in the joy of new beginnings. I've lit candles before walking out the door to every important milestone in my life, and I once even brought an Uber driver upstairs to light a candle for his father (sorry about bringing a stranger into my home, Mom). It's a wonder I haven't burned the house down. Thank God for the holy angels protecting me from accidental arson.

Seriously, though, for me, that candle station is a visible symbol of an invisible force that has been guiding me for my entire life—my faith in God. And those flickering candles are reminders to be intentional with my prayers and to be of service to others. My life is built on that faith, and it's what I've turned to and relied upon for as long as I can remember. You may know from my podcast that I am a practicing Catholic, which simply means that's how I choose to express my faith and walk on my spiritual journey. But I want to be very clear on this point—I do not believe Catholicism is the *only* way to exercise faith in God or something bigger than you. In fact, I do not believe that it's always religion in general that helps us lead a deeply spiritual life. We are all spiritual beings and that can mean different things for different people. Faith is *very* personal, and it's important to discover what that means for you, and how to connect with your innate spirituality in your own way.

Living faithfully is hard, though; there's no question about that. My mind is literally a battlefield, and the war playing out is between my human nature—which is influenced and swayed by earthly things like fear—and my spiritual nature—which knows something bigger is in control. We all need something to keep us from getting lost when we're being tossed around by the waves of this life. And boy, have I been tossed around . . . but it's faith that has saved me more times than I can count.

From the time I was a little child I've had faith. Growing up I'd seen God in so many undeniable ways in my life that it's almost like I can't *not* have faith. The truth is, everything you have read about me and my struggles in this book—letting go of attachments, creating balance, quieting my fear—has come down to having faith. So, how do I still lose my way sometimes?

I think it's because too often we bow to these things that are smaller than us, these petty worries and fears, even though we want to be people of faith. We don't mean to, we don't even want to, but we do it anyway. But over time instead of beating myself up about it I've come to realize that it's okay. Part of our spiritual journey is thankfully full of grace. When I find myself getting all worked up, I light a candle, say a prayer, and then let that mental chatter go quiet. Then, when the worries start to come back, I remember that I'm determined to live a different way, so I do it all over again.

There have been many dark times when I have turned to my faith in complete surrender and basically said, *I don't know why this is happening, and I don't know what to do next, but I know you will guide me. I am here, begging. Please show me the way.* And without fail, I have been guided out of the darkness. Divinely led back to light. For me, the key is that I have been *led*—I've allowed myself to be led by God, rather than trying to control everything myself.

Still, despite all the times I have felt led or guided, I forget. I find myself reverting back to relying solely on myself, especially when I'm stressed-out or when I feel untethered. I've been stuck in the anxiousness of a moment, overwhelmed by all that life piles on.

On the other hand, I've experienced a sense of peace that seems to come from outside of myself. So, to me, the question becomes how do we access that calmer, more spiritually connected state of mind on a regular basis? How can we operate from that spacc rather than from being one breath away from out of control?

The goal isn't to create a life that doesn't have obstacles, or to try and control our each and every reaction to those obstacles along the way. Quitc thc oppositc. The goal is to *remember* or even *re-remember* my faith as much as I can, and to depend on it to get me over the obstacles that life puts in front of me, or that I've put in front of myself. When I remember my faith, my recovery time gets shorter and whatever problem I'm dealing with isn't as likely to steal my joy or to bleed into every area of my life. It's all in that remembering. If

I remember my faith, it does a lot for me in return—*it* reminds *me* to find my center again and to give myself to something larger than me.

I have some specific practices that help me do just that. I have intentionally woven these tools into my daily life because they strengthen my faith and keep my spiritual connection alive. They remind me of the undercurrent of faith that flows through my own life. I share them in the hopes that they will inspire you to find, rekindle, or create some tools of your own so that you can always renew your spirit too, especially at times when the pressures of the world knock you off your path.

Lighting Candles

When I need to rediscover stillness in my mind because I'm overthinking, worrying, and doubting, lighting a candle and praying quietly is one of the places I can find it. For me, there is so much power in the solitary act of igniting a flame for an intention, or someone else's intention. It stays lit even when my messy mind takes over and my prayers get buried by my mental load. My prayer remains, even when I do not. Sometimes I do this at home, at my candle station, but often I go to a church, even when no one else is there. And I always leave feeling renewed and settled, like I'm walking on solid earth again.

I have come to realize that the candle lighting is also about stillness and focus and giving myself the opportunity to connect with my spirit and to get centered. It focuses my energy in one direction. For some people, going on a walk or run could accomplish the same thing. Or silently meditating in a quiet room with no distractions. The point is to find an activity that helps you silence the thoughts in your head so that you can let your spirit take charge. The act of lighting a candle is like taking a quick off-ramp from that speeding highway of nonstop thought. It lets me slow down, and then hand the wheel back to God.

Asking for Signs

Signs are everywhere, but our spiritual eyes must be open in order to see them for what they are. I think sometimes we want to brush signs off like they're just coincidence. But signs are spiritual gifts given to us, meant to encourage us and propel us forward in life.

Purple roses. 333. Yellow birds. "Let It Be." These are all signs that I've asked for and seen at pivotal moments in my life. Ever since I was a child, I've seen signs. They guide me in the right direction, or away from the wrong one. But I'm not any more gifted in noticing signs than anyone else. I believe we *all* have the ability to see signs given to us by God. We simply have to ask for them and then be open to receiving them.

Like I often do when I'm diving into something new, when I first started writing this book I put too much pressure on myself. So, on the day I began writing, rather than getting caught up in the weight of it all, I asked for a clear sign that the Holy Spirit would be present while I wrote. The simple act of asking for the sign gave me faith in my faith and reminded me that I don't have to do it by myself. And wow, did I ever receive the sign I asked for.

I grabbed a book of daily readings that was sitting in a basket beside my candles. I decided to flip to my son Shepherd's birthday, September 17, and when I opened to the page, my knees buckled. It was an image of St. Hildegard, a Benedictine nun who was a writer. Depicted in this illustration, she was writing a book with the Holy Spirit in a cloud above her head as she wrote. *A woman writing a book with the Holy Spirit in a cloud above her head*, for crying out loud. I mean, can you imagine a clearer sign? It gave me an overwhelming sense that I was being guided and I was headed in the right direction. That was no coincidence.

You've probably felt something similar too, maybe without even asking for it. Was there ever a time that you felt lost or unsure, and then something appeared in your life that was undeniable, making it easier to rest assured that you were moving in the right direction? It might've been something completely unexpected or out of the ordinary, but it just gave you a sense of peace and confirmation. I think of those as signs too.

Sometimes there are signs that show up again and again; I don't even have to ask for them. An example is the song "Let It Be" by the Beatles. Any time I'm about to do something big in my life, I'll hear that song, pretty much without fail. It'll show up in the most random of moments and playlists, there to give me that little nudge I need.

On the day I first met the woman who would become my literary agent, we connected at a coffee shop off the beaten path in Nashville. I was newly married and charting the path for my career. Also, I had found out I was pregnant with my first child the day before. I had always known I would one day write a book, so this felt very much like a "stars aligned" kind of meeting. But I wondered about the timing and needed some reassurance. My would-be agent began telling me about the book she felt I was already writing, just based on what she saw in my social media content. It was like she was reading my mind.

The whole time we'd been in there talking, I hadn't heard any music. Maybe I'd just been deep in thought, I don't know. But as we were making our way toward the door, "Let It Be" started playing. I heard it—loud and clear.

Signs on Our Behalf

I've also learned that signs can also show up on our behalf through other people. When I was in my third year of competing in Miss Kentucky, I was a mess. I'd worked so hard, poured all of myself into it. In the Miss America system, there is an age limit of twenty-five, and I was about to hit it. I am a competitive person and I'd gone so deep into winning mode that I almost burned myself out on the whole thing. In the final weeks leading up to the move-in day for the weeklong competition, my mind was spinning out of control. I was feeling the pressure to be perfect and I was intensely aware that this was my last shot to win—and I had to win. I was suddenly and profoundly confused. *Was I even supposed to do this? Did I really want to win it? Should I just walk away?* I called my mom and through heavy sobs, I told her I didn't know what I should do.

Now, at that specific moment, my mom was with my youngest brother on a trip to Washington, D.C. She was listening to me cry on the other end of the phone, not sure how to respond. Often, she just says whatever she thinks, but I think that time she knew she needed to be intentional with her words. I remember her saying, "Hang on, the whole class just walked into the National Cathedral, and I need to go with them. I'll call you right back." Trying to compose myself, I let her go.

She called me back that night and she had a whole new clarity. Unwavering in her tone, she encouraged me and told me to keep my head up and not to give up. "You can do this. You were meant to do this," she said. "Don't get in your own way here at the end. Keep pushing through." It helped me so much having her reassuring words in my head. The clouds in my mind seemed to part, and I kept moving forward.

A couple of weeks after that, I won Miss Kentucky. And later, when all the excitement had calmed down, I asked my mom about that phone call. I asked her why she was so sure. She told me that when she had been standing on the steps of the cathedral, she didn't know what the right answer was, or what I should do. She prayed before she went in and asked God to send her a clear sign to know what to do as a parent of a struggling child. She walked all the way to the front and knelt down, then she looked up. When she lifted her eyes to the mosaic above the altar, she saw an image of brightly arranged tiles of Jesus placing a crown on Mary's head and it read "On her head will be placed a crown." And that was all she needed. She knew. And it was the resolve in the tone of her voice when she called me back that I needed to hear; it snapped me back into focus.

No Sign Is Also a Sign

If you've never seen a sign, or you say, "That never happens for me. I could never see things like that," that's what will happen. The words we speak about ourselves become who we are. But it works the other way around too. If you start to look for signs, they'll be all around you. Belief is what opens our spiritual eyes.

So, what about those times when you take the risk, you ask for the sign, you keep your heart and mind open, and then . . . nothing? Silence. *Hello, God? Are you there? Where's my sign?* There have been plenty of times when I've found myself asking, begging for signs over and over because I wanted to validate what I wanted, but then I don't see it anywhere. It's really hard, I know. *Sometimes the lack of the sign is the answer we've been looking for.* It's tough because we want so badly to believe that our choice, our decision, our chosen path is the right one. The battle between our will and God's will is an age-old struggle. But it's always amazing to me how quickly the right direction becomes clear once I've accepted I was headed in the wrong one. The sooner I let go of the idea I had in mind, the sooner I get to the miracle.

YOUR SPIRITUAL AWARENESS

While each journey of faith is individual, just like each journey of self-improvement is individual, we all have tools we can use along the way. You may already know what works for you, so consider this your reminder to use them more. We *all* have the capacity for faith, but it's something we must work at. I could write all day long about the many times I've seen signs I desperately needed, and had prayers answered, but I still begin to drift if I am not intentional. I still slip back into old habits, grab on to the reins of my life once again, and I forget to maintain that spiritual connection.

Life will pull and tug at us from every direction. Distractions stream in and our brains are overwrought, exhausted from split focus. And within that exhausted state, we often reach for quick hits from the world in order to feel aligned, rather than tapping into the ever-present spring that is right in front of us.

Faith is like breathing for me; it is as important as oxygen. But just as it's so easy to take the unconscious act of breathing for granted, it's easy to take faith for granted, and to forget that it is, in fact, what is sustaining our life.

If you haven't paid much attention to your spiritual self, are you feeling that internal tug to explore it? Are you wondering if perhaps there is more for you in this realm that you've been blind to? I encourage you to discover simple, everyday ways you can expand upon your innate spirituality. Just open your mind to it like you would anything else.

And realize that even if you already consider yourself a strong person of faith, there is always room for growth. Don't stop seeking just because you think you've checked off all the boxes of a particular religion. Spirituality is a route, not a routine.

There is a way to live differently. And just like living fully, it's choosing to live faith*fully*.

CHAPTER 10

Ordinary Joy

The Simple Life? The only simple life I was interested in for the majority of my years spent as a prisoner to achievement was the one Paris Hilton and Nicole Richie were living on reality television. They would leave their glamorous LA existence to go and stay on a farm or in a small town with "simple" strangers and live their more average way of life, all while being filmed for a TV show. Simple, small, average—these were the *last* things I wanted in the life I was creating—that is, until I woke up.

Now, even when I'm sitting in a lobby in some big city waiting for some big meeting, I'm usually scrolling through Pinterest looking at chicken coops that I want in my backyard so I can collect my own eggs one day. I crave the ordinary joys of a simpler life.

That's because I learned from experience that the payoff for success was always so quick and not nearly as joy-filled as I expected it to be, especially as compared to the drudgery of the road it took to get there. I figured out, *finally*, that more and more brought me less and less. That bigger things out there weren't necessarily creating bigger joy in me. But it took me a large chunk of my life to see that. I wish I could have taken a shortcut so I didn't have to lose that valuable time chasing things I wouldn't even like once I obtained them.

When I was going from school to school speaking to students, I did a question and answer portion at the end. I always asked the kids what they wanted to be when they grew up. *Every single child* born after the year 2000 said they wanted to be a basketball player, a singer, an actress, and some just cut to the chase and said they wanted to be famous. Oddly enough, "famous" is an actual job these days. I'd say 5 percent of the kids aspired to a more traditional profession—a teacher or a doctor—but it was typically followed by "oh, and a rock star." Like the other things didn't count, they weren't enough to stand on their own.

That belief sticks with us, even as we get to be adults and realize there are only like fifteen people chosen for an NBA basketball team and only one Lady Gaga. As we continue on our more normal paths, we feel it's like *The Wizard of Oz* in reverse, everything slowly fading back to black-and-white. We begin to feel average, normal, small, and worst of all, sad about it. Sad about our lives. Sad about the type of life that, in my opinion, provides the easiest access to the ordinary joy we all crave.

Too often, we search for our bliss in bigger places. In grander things—bigger houses, another promotion. How can you keep your eyes on your path when you're always focused on the horizon? You can't. Rather than reaching, stretching, needing, and desiring more, bigger, and better somewhere out there in the future, we can start looking around us and seeing the splendor within our current view.

So, I decided to make a shift to focus on ordinary joy, and to stop seeking it in places I knew I couldn't find it. I also gave myself permission to find it in the places the world told me I wouldn't find it. I started to move away from the constant, addictive need for hits of happiness and toward a life where I could feel fulfilled in the everyday, ordinary happenings.

Glimmers of Joy

I remember the day like it was yesterday. It was early in the morning when I took the long drive through the yellow-and-red-blanketed mountains of eastern Kentucky to the Trimble County Apple Festival. It was a typical occurrence in my daily obligations as the representative for my state, but this day felt different. The air was cool and crisp as I stood outside the courthouse dragging my hands across a white picnic table displaying ten of the best apple pies in the county. I don't know why they chose the person on the strictest diet to judge the apple pie–eating contest that day, but maybe that's why they tasted so good.

I judged a local pageant next, then moved on to the arts and crafts tents, where I perused crocheted blankets, handmade pottery, lace doilies, jellies, and breads. Ordinary things that brought other people joy. And I remember the sun's rays diffusing through the tents, like a shimmering shower of light.

There was something about that day—connecting with strangers, the beautiful setting—that gave me such zeal, zeal that I can still feel when I recall the details now. It was the happiest day, so normal, so ordinary. But the whole day was filled with golden glimmers of joy.

That's when I started to realize, the simple life was no longer something I wanted to avoid. Instead, it became what I aspired to live each and every day. Finding those simple, ordinary joys that come in abundance when we are living fully. It took me a while to fully embrace the simple life, but the seeds were planted that day.

Choosing Your Own Version of Joy

Our simple, everyday existence is where life happens. I'm sure you've heard that before, but this is where the majority of our time on earth is spent—in the everyday. So, mastering the art of appreciating the everyday and squeezing joy out of regular life—if you can master this, you're almost guaranteed a happier existence.

But first you must recognize which of these ordinary things give you life. For me, it's a long list. Planting the flowers in my summer flower box, and cooking for my family. If I were to write down my bliss list, it would include Christmas lights, the ocean, the smell of babies, the first hints of fall . . . and on and on.

It's different for everyone. My dad is a mountain climber—not just any mountain climber, but like an *all in* one. I'm talking Everest a couple of times, the seven summits. When he was sixty years old, he blurted out that he was going to climb the seven highest summits in the world. As I write this book, only a little over four hundred people have done this, actually summited the seven highest peaks on all seven continents. And of them, only a handful were over sixty when they began. People ask him all the time why in the world he would want to climb through the blistering cold, through deadly terrain, sleeping out in the elements for three months . . . as a hobby. In their opinion, he should be playing golf, enjoying retirement, relishing all he's created. Instead, he's sleeping in a tent in thirty degrees below zero next to a fellow climber, with hot water bottles between them, just trying not to freeze to death. But that's his joy!

He doesn't just love getting to the summit; he loves the prepping, the packing, unpacking, choosing what kind of merino wool clothing to include. . . . In pursuit of a dream or a goal, he's finding joy in the everyday moments that most people wouldn't find pleasure in. Sometimes it's such a grind when we're on our way toward our goals. We think it's all about putting our head down—work, work, work. But it's a win-win if you can live your life well while in the pursuit of these things. It's not only the summit moment that matters to him; it's also the process of getting there. That's how it should be for all of us.

While he's on each climb, he writes lessons to grandkids. He started this on his very first expedition, when he was feeling guilty being so far away when I was going to be giving birth to his first grandchild, Ford. He writes these lessons with a pencil and paper, since you can't exactly bring a laptop to the top of Everest. And the ink in pens freezes at such extreme temperatures.

He says that every continent has a different culture, and he always learns something about himself from the mountains, but also something about the world. The people he's with while climbing are also a part of the treasure he takes with him. Here's an excerpt from one of the lessons he wrote:

> Don't let anyone define happiness for you. Many people don't understand what I see in climbing or how it can make anyone happy. It is cold, little oxygen, a long way from home, expensive and dangerous. No two humans are alike, so why should we have one definition of happiness? *We must define what makes us happy. If not, society will do it for us and we will always fall short.*

You see, if you don't *know* what makes you happy, then you'll just follow what "they" think should make you happy. If my dad did that, he'd be the most miserable retiree on the golf course. We have to do our own deciding. Don't let others point you in a direction of false desires. *You will never find joy in a life you didn't choose.*

Don't Be a Joy-eur

One of the reasons I think people get so obsessed with social media is because they are searching for joy outside of their immediate lives. We are a society of joy voyeurs. We watch other people, many of whom are wealthy, famous, and beautiful, living these extraordinary lives and we think those are the keys to their happiness.

The truth is, we don't know if those people are happy at all. And spending a life solely in pursuit of extreme wealth, fame, or beauty is the very definition of wasting a life. That mentality enslaves us to try to achieve the unachievable. It's never enough to satisfy, and we become bottomless pits, never filled up, always needing more.

Besides, it's the *feeling* we're really after anyway, not the things. What we crave is the sensation of joy flowing in and through us—that head-to-toe flood of happiness we experience, like when a child first sees what's waiting for them under the Christmas tree. And that feeling is a heck of a lot more accessible to us than the object we think will produce it. It's a whole lot easier to make a pot of chili (or whatever it is that brings you that feeling) than to make ten million dollars. My point is we can have that feeling right now; it's right in front of us.

Once I realized the things that brought me joy, I knew I needed to create more time and space for them. And I had to stop listening to the outside world when it questioned my choices. This was hard for me; it still is sometimes. There's this fear of being small, of living a life that appears to be black-and-white. But the truth is, a simpler life is not a life in black-and-white, it's a life full of color.

Find what makes you happy in your everyday life rather than looking right past it all, singularly focused on obtaining more. What are those things for you? What is your very own bliss list composed of? It doesn't have to be an expensive or extravagant experience like a fancy dinner out or a tropical vacation. I'm talking about planning to take an hour-long soak in the tub listening to your favorite audiobook. Or lunch with that friend who always makes you laugh. Find what those things are, and then get started creating your own ordinary joy.

Taking the time to reflect upon the answers can give you the power to discover and connect with your ordinary joys, even the ones that already exist in your everyday life. I firmly believe there is potential for an abundant life in the things we already have; we simply have to open our eyes to it. And then if something doesn't fit, redefine what joy is for you now.

Happiness is not a gift from another person, or a destination on a map, or a point in the distant future of your life; it is a choice you make in the present moment. The question is, will you choose it?

CHAPTER 11

Good Lord, It's Morning

Ding, ding! The little bell at the top of the doorway into my grandparents' store rang, and the first customer of the day entered. It was still dark outside—the kind of inky dark that covers the earth in those final hours of night before daylight begins to break. Most people would be asleep, warm in their bed, but I watched as my grandma stood behind the counter of Bud's Country Corner, her eyes bright. "Good morning, Tommy. What'll it be today?" she asked in her familiar voice.

The corners of Tommy's mouth were turned slightly downward as he mindlessly rubbed his neck. "I'll do the bacon, egg, and cheese, ma'am." And at that, my grandma turned toward the griddle behind her and got busy assembling the homemade breakfast sandwich. There were rows of buttered burger buns, hot bacon, sausage patties, and fried eggs, all prepared and ready to be served up. Expertly wielding the spatula, she put the sandwich together and wrapped it in aluminum foil like she'd done countless times before. As she did—ding, ding, ding, ding—the front doorbell rang over and over as dozens more men, dressed just like Tommy, started pouring in. Once inside, they all lined up patiently, still trying to wake up after yet another short night's sleep.

Handing Tommy his sandwich, my grandma looked at him and said, "Just remember. You've got two choices. You can either say 'Good morning, Lord!' or 'Good Lord, it's morning!' " Tommy mustered up a little bit of a smile as he took the sandwich along with the wisdom, and gave her a nod.

"Good morning, Lord. I suppose. You have a great day, ma'am." And he turned to take a seat at the white plastic table that would soon be filled with familiar faces and clouds of cigarette smoke.

This was the typical scene for several decades at my grandparents' little country store in rural Kentucky. It was the essential starting point for every coal miner's morning until my grandparents sold it, once they were approaching their eighties. Like clockwork, every day of the week at 4:30 a.m., local miners and farmers showed up as if following a homing beacon. It was probably the brightest spot in their day, when both their stomachs and their spirits were fed before heading to the mines and the fields.

My grandmother knew from experience that the way we approach our lives plays a giant role in how we feel. She was one of the earliest living, breathing examples of chosen optimism that I ever encountered, and she still is today. With the way she lives her life, she has taught me one of the most valuable lessons a person can learn: perspective is everything.

The Process of Perspective

Have you ever found yourself greeting the day with a heavy sigh, thinking about the drudgery ahead, your bottomless to-do list, with very little joy in your heart? Maybe it's not an everyday sentiment, but once in a while? It's okay; I do it too. We've all been in slumps. Life is filled with peaks and valleys, and shifting your perspective can be a powerful tool for pulling yourself out of a valley.

To truly do so, however, requires more intention and action than a simple decision to look on the bright side of any given circumstance. It starts from the moment we open our eyes each morning. We can greet the day or let the day greet us. We can roll over and immediately grab the phone, scan through emails, check the news, and get sucked into the madness. Or we can make different choices that can change the tone of our entire day, greeting the day on our terms instead.

I know morning routines are personal. Different habits work for different people, but I guarantee scrolling through a list of to-do's while still lying in bed is going to feel a lot different from setting your feet on the floor, feeling the ground beneath you, picturing the day going your way, and greeting the day with gladness.

One of the most influential things in setting the course of our lives in a better direction is setting our days in a better direction, because days make up a life. So don't underestimate the significance of shifting something as simple as your morning—it can have powerful, lasting effects.

One way I've learned to shift my morning is by jotting down to-do lists at night. I like to create a list at night so it gives me a leg up on the next day and a plan to help things run smoothly. In that list, I sometimes even plan things in specific blocks of time. This allows me to go to bed with a clear head, but it also gives me a better shot at not slipping into a negative mindset the next morning because I have a clear game plan.

The other way I create the right tone for the day is to remind myself that I can choose my pace. In other words, I don't always have to be in such a huge hurry. I think there's a reason why haste and waste are almost the same word. Why the only thing distinguishing one from the other is a single letter. Because to me, they could be interchangeable. I've learned this from experience.

I spent half a lifetime hurrying around, making haste. Trying to go faster, get there quicker, grow faster, have a family and a house and another whatever faster. Then I got it all. But I didn't stop running the race. I kept right on rushing from one thing to the next, one goal to the next. I found myself rushing my children to put on their shoes and get out the door, rushing to the grocery store, through a workout, through days of book writing, and sometimes through holidays. Have you ever said this crazy thing? "Well, we just need to get through Christmas then we'll be able to handle that." I mean, who really wants to rush through the magic of *Christmas*?

When I pull back and gain some perspective, I always realize I need to slow down. What the heck am I doing, hurrying to the grave? It's a wild thing to constantly be obsessed with moving faster. But I have come to see that it is also a thing that wastes a life. And I am determined not to allow that to happen.

It takes discipline to live slower. It's hard for me, and it might be for you too. It's a fast-paced world we are living in. My therapist has pointed out that I tend to live with one foot on the gas and the other on the brakes. I definitely do that. I'll even rush to slow down, which isn't actually slowing down at all. But by the grace of God, I've learned to slow down a little. I know that I love living life too much to waste my energy rushing through it. So, especially lately, I've been letting my foot off the gas ever so slightly. And it feels really good to slow the pace.

I'll always have to keep a watchful eye on my inner speedometer and remember that life isn't about getting to a destination faster. So, the next time it's pouring rain outside, instead of grabbing an umbrella and racing through my tasks, I'm going to opt to play in the muddy puddles with my sons. A tiny choice, but that's all it takes.

DON'T LISTEN TO THE WARNINGS

Before I had my first son, Ford, everyone would tell me, "Oh, enjoy your sleep while you can," or "you'll never eat at a restaurant again," or "enjoy your time as a couple because that's almost over." I think people say these things not out of a sincere desire to give advice, but rather because it's easy to articulate negative things. It's easy to put into words what it's like to be up all night with a crying baby and potty training a toddler at the same time. But for some reason, it's harder to find a way to describe the feeling you get when you see that baby smile at you first thing in the morning.

I didn't hear much from anyone I know about how awesome the toddler phase is. How fun it is to see your child become more self-sufficient, to hear them learning to communicate or step into the role of a big sibling. Instead, every single story was about the massive meltdown in public or the terrible twos, or the sibling rivalry, or something else that goes along with this phase of life. The "Good Lord, it's morning" stories are somehow easier to tell.

If I had let people's warnings and negativity frame how I feel about parenting, I'd be in a mess of trouble. My dad says the same thing about mountaineering. If he listened to every horror story from the mountainside, every tale of someone slipping into a crevasse and having to be rescued, or sleeping on an ice block at forty below, well, he'd probably hang up his gear and pick up a new hobby. But he doesn't let that stuff affect his outlook on climbing. When we think about and revel in all of the fun, rewarding, exciting parts, the other stuff doesn't feel like such a big deal. It's all about choosing to focus on the good.

Another season of life when people tend to give these kinds of warnings is moving into adulthood. Maybe it's as your college experience is coming to an end or before you're about to start your first job. You'll often hear, "Enjoy those days while you can, because once you're living in the real world, the fun is all over." But the truth is, all the actual fun stuff occurs in the real world. A lot of life's big challenges and milestones happen in those adult years. Plus, if you choose to look at it that way, and believe that the real world is an uphill battle, then that's the reality you'll create for yourself. There are exciting parts of young adulthood, sure, but the adventure doesn't end there. Not even close.

When you want to manifest good things to be positive most of the time, reality will get in the way sometimes. There's disappointment in these tough moments, but there's double disappointment when you focus on the negative and overlook the good aspects too.

Choosing Not to Dig in Our Heels

I think we'd all agree it's easier to have a positive outlook when things are going well, but what about maintaining a positive outlook when things don't go according to our expectations? It's not easy, but I believe it's essential.

The night before I was supposed to be heading off to college at Miami University in Oxford, Ohio, my dad said, "You probably need to pack different clothes because I already paid your first-semester tuition at a different school and that's where you're going." Um, what? I already had my scan card, I'd met my roommate, and we'd gotten matching bedspreads and curtains. I'd bought my books and taken care of every other detail, right down to my dorm room refrigerator. It was a done deal. Except, apparently, it wasn't.

My dad is not the kind of dad who makes decisions for me. He never has been. In fact, I can't remember any other time that he's done anything like that. But he felt so strongly about this. He knew in his heart that I belonged at a different college, one that was smaller and closer to home and to Nashville, where I was going back and forth for singing and music. So, yes, being the resourceful man that he is, my dad took all of the necessary steps to fully enroll me at Sewanee, where I'd been accepted but didn't want to go after I'd taken a tour, all without my knowledge . . . until that moment.

I admit, I didn't handle the news gracefully at first. I was mad and told my dad, "As soon as I get there, I'm packing up and leaving." But he stood his ground. You can imagine, it was such a shock and I needed some time to absorb the new plan. I was supposed to move in to Sewanee the next day. That night was filled with so much anxiety. *This is going to be awful,* I thought. I didn't talk to my dad. I begged my mom. But to no avail. I packed and got ready, but I was sure I'd leave school the minute my parents dropped me off at campus and drove away. But somehow, when I got to Sewanee, something in me changed. I decided I'd at least keep an open mind. I decided I wasn't going to dig in my heels and determine to be miserable just so I could prove my dad wrong. Because I knew that wouldn't hurt anyone but me. Instead, I opted for optimism.

I might have envisioned my path going toward one place, but suddenly, there I was in a totally different situation than I had expected. And when I looked around, I realized it was pretty great. It didn't take long before I saw that I did belong there. I had an amazing experience at the college, and I'm really glad it worked out the way it did. It was definitely the best decision I *never* made.

I'm not saying you should always listen when decisions are made for you. Not at all. But for those times in life when you've wound up somewhere you didn't originally aim to go, try first to change your perspective before you decide to dig your heels in and be miserable just because you're angry or sad or frustrated at having arrived there. Trying to prove the world wrong is a pointless pursuit that will only cause you pain. We can't always control where we end up, but we can control how we choose to look at it.

Don't Get Addicted to Low-Energy Thoughts

I've noticed I can't maintain a "Good morning, Lord!" perspective when I choose to stay disappointed if things don't go the way I want. I can easily get derailed by every complication—big and small—that pops up in my day. Over time, I might succumb so often to low-energy thinking it can become like an addiction. It can choke out my ability to keep a better outlook if I choose a negative one on a regular basis. And, just like with any addiction, even though I know it's keeping me from living an incredible life and I want to fix it, I feel like I can't. Like it's hopeless. So I keep looking at things through a negative lens, expecting a different result but never getting one. That's a classic cycle of addiction.

Look at your life and your circumstances right now. Is your inner monologue set to a negative autopilot and it's flying you right into the ground? When something doesn't meet your expectations, do you immediately start losing altitude? You've got to acknowledge that *you're* flying that plane, and the minute you start pulling back on those controls, you can pull yourself out of that rapid descent.

I have days when I wake up thinking *How am I going to be a good mom, do all these things in my business, be a good spouse, and take time for myself?* But I cast out that low-energy story and rewrite it to reflect how thankful I am to have these things in my life. I say, "I'm grateful for all these opportunities. And I'm grateful that I have two children seventeen months apart. Yes, we're in the thick of it right now, but they'll always have each other. I'm also grateful I have a spouse who is willing to work together and I get to spend time with him, even on my busiest days." I create that internal shift.

When people ask me how I maintain a positive point of view and bounce back when something threatens to derail me, I tell them it's because I've seen it work out before. I have all this proof that it will be okay, so I'm able to grab hold of that positive perspective and apply it.

When you overcome obstacles in your life, you begin to talk to and *about* yourself differently. Regardless of what's happening to you or around you, the choice is still yours. You can choose to rewrite the script of your day and replace those low-energy thoughts. The more you put this into practice, you'll be able to talk about yourself in that way too, which in turn creates a lot of momentum in the right direction.

For the times when I do get stuck in negative thoughts or disappointment when reality doesn't match my expectations, I do what I think of as an emergency prayer. It's like a grounding prayer, where I ask God to help me turn this around because I want to do the best work I possibly can, and I don't want this to stand in my way. It goes something like, "Please enter into this situation. I need you here in my life, now. I cannot do this on my own." Then I have faith in the process and know that every negative or hard thing leads somewhere positive in my life. That allows me to release the low-energy thinking and shift my entire perspective.

PUTTING PERSPECTIVE INTO PRACTICE

When you do peel back all of your layers and get to the heart of your perspective on life, what do you find there? Do your thoughts often return to how insurmountable your problems feel? Or how much you regret something in your past? Maybe you sometimes wish things could be different for you. Or that life isn't fair, and that you were just born with bad luck. Maybe you subscribe to the "everything that can go wrong will go wrong" outlook on life. Well, if you say and believe everything will go wrong, then of course it will. It's like when you're riding a bike—you have to look where you want to go. If you're looking at a ditch, you're going to steer yourself right into it. But you can begin to change it all if you shift your perspective.

Starting now, you can choose a "Good morning, Lord!" outlook instead.

CHAPTER 12

Hocus-Pocus?

I was eight years old and looking through thick, round glasses at a plastic first-place trophy in a box at River Days, a festival in the town where my mom grew up. I sat there while a lot of other kids in the talent show were begging for corn dogs and to play games to win a goldfish, but not me. I was fixated on the trophy. I pictured myself holding it on the stage in my red fringe jacket, cowboy boots, and hat. I pictured myself walking off the stage with it. I pictured it on my shelf at home. It was already mine; I simply had to go through the motions of getting to it. Very competitive for an eight-year-old, but even at that early age, I knew what I wanted. And at the end of that day, I won first place. That was the first time I ever visualized something, even though I didn't know that's what I was doing.

As I have shifted from posting ideas in beauty, fashion, and lifestyle into sharing content about living a bigger life, I noticed one very specific hot topic with my followers: visualization. Or as others call it, manifesting. I don't know exactly why so many people ask about this more than a lot of other topics I discuss. Maybe it's such a popular idea because it represents a quicker path to instant gratification. Or maybe it feels like an easier road. Perhaps it feels like magic. Whatever the appeal, I've been visualizing what I want for my life since I was a little girl, and it's one of the few things that hasn't lost its power as I've grown into the woman I am today.

Oftentimes, things that seem a little bit out-there can be polarizing; they either draw people in and speak to their sense of curiosity, or they deter people completely. The first time I talked about visualization to my sister, she said, "Uh, Mal, I want to do that, but I feel like a crazy person." Funny at the time, but it does represent a common sentiment. If you fall into that category like my sister did, don't dismiss the idea right away—give this concept a chance.

Maybe this is the first time you're hearing about the idea of manifesting, or maybe you're like I was, and you've been doing it for years and just not calling it that. Wherever you're coming from, it's available to you for free. And it can bring you a pretty spectacular life if you don't write it off as hocus-pocus.

Now, the concept of visualization or manifesting is pretty basic. Simply put, it's envisioning specific things and bringing them into the reality of your life. It can be anything. Physical things—like, say, you want to get healthy and fit, or material things—your dream home and dream job. Or it could be manifesting your perfect life partner. You can even manifest a feeling, such as joy or high energy. Manifesting is bringing these things you want into your life. And there are several ways to do it.

First, though, you must begin by not being afraid to ask for what you truly want. Then you have to feel confident enough to envision yourself receiving it. Like I did with that trophy at just eight years old. Of course, there is work required to then make it happen; I don't just ask for something and then sit down and wait for it to arrive at my doorstep. I work for it too. But all of that work begins with a vision inside my head.

My best friend, Shawn Johnson, won an Olympic gold medal in gymnastics when she was sixteen. As you can imagine, rising to that level of expertise in any sport requires a *lot* of training and very strict mental discipline. But what's wild is, one day Shawn and I were talking about visualizing and she said, "Oh, I did that with the Olympics too."

"What?" I asked. "How in the world would you visualize that level of training?"

Shawn explained to me how she trained hours and hours less than a lot of the young athletes she competed against. Her coach would allow her to leave the gym having done fewer reps, routines, and runs through than the other girls so she could go home, lie in bed, and envision her routine over and over. She said each time she made a mistake in her mental routine she would start it over, at the beginning. She told me what she learned is how hard it is for your mind to envision things going perfectly right; its default is the opposite, actually.

I've read countless stories like this about athletes in almost every sport, and it just shows the power our minds have over our bodies and, really, the world around us. That very same power Shawn utilized to win the gold medal in one of the most competitive sports in the world is available to you too, and you can apply it toward anything you want in life.

How I Visualize and Manifest

I use all sorts of methods to visualize—vision boards, affirmations, writing notes in my phone—about the things that I want to come to fruition—but as if they've already happened. I have put a piece of paper on my vision board with an exact amount I want in my savings account by the end of the year, or a vacation spot or a health goal or faith goal, and they've almost all come true.

You may be thinking, *sounds easy for you, Mallory, you've been doing this forever*. But you can unleash the power of visualization in your own life too. The book *The Secret* is a great resource on manifesting for a beginner. It gives a lot of detail and specific examples, so if you're looking for a deep dive, you can start there. But in terms of an overview of manifesting, it's pretty easy; I think you'll be surprised. It starts by getting into the right mind-set. If you approach it as a total skeptic, and you're just testing the theory in order to disprove it, then that's exactly what you'll do. On the other hand, if you open your mind and heart completely, and decide you are going to trust the process, then you greatly increase the odds of attracting what you want in your life. Openness is a requirement, which means believing that you *can* and *will* receive what you visualize.

1. First, think about what you want to bring into your life, making sure your goals are aligned with your specific vision of living fully. Maybe it's a specific job, or a life you dream of in a different city.

2. Then choose how you are going to visualize it. I find it best to create something tangible that I can keep within my line of sight on a regular basis as a visible reminder of what I'm manifesting.
   - A vision board might feel like the right method for you. If so, you can go old-school and get some poster board and start taping or gluing photos, words, cutouts, printouts, etc., on there until you

have a physical reflection of the vision in your mind. Or you can make a virtual vision board. But—and this is important—if you don't really believe you can bring something into your life, don't stick it on your vision board. It has to be something that you 100 percent believe you can have. Note: you don't have to figure out all the details of how you will get it, just believe you will actually have it.

- Are you more of a writer and prefer to write out what you're visualizing? You can write it in a journal, on a piece of paper taped somewhere that you'll see it often, or in your phone, whatever works for you.

3. Next, you'll need to get specific! Think about and envision every single detail of this thing you are bringing into your life. For instance:
   - Is it a spouse? Think about the exact traits that you want in that spouse. You can even think about the way that they look. Visualize yourself in that life, with that spouse. What does it feel like, what does it look like?
   - Is it a home? Picture yourself in the hallways; picture yourself hanging art on the wall. Find any sort of image that looks like this home that you want and put that on your vision board.

4. Finally, see yourself receiving it and living your life with it. Act as if it has already happened. I think of visualizing as prayer in fast-

forward, like the prayer has already been answered. So, even before it is yours, be grateful for it. Let those feelings take root inside of you. Know that it will come to pass in your life.

Dealing with Sabotaging Thoughts

When I first heard this whole notion of bringing things into my life in this way, I started thinking, *Oh, shoot, I can't control my thoughts like that.* I have a lot of negative thoughts come into my mind on a regular basis, and sometimes they set up shop there before I even realize it. Maybe you know what I mean; we think about worst-case scenarios all the time. I'd think, *Oh my gosh, I'm going to manifest all these terrible things in my life.* But I know it takes many more bad thoughts to manifest something bad in your life than it takes good thoughts to manifest something good. That gives me the confidence to keep practicing manifesting without fear of doing it wrong.

But I will tell you those incessant negative thoughts can sabotage all the work you put into manifesting amazing things in your life, so start paying attention to your thoughts. It's so easy for them to come in. Thoughts like "I hate my job," and "I'm never going to be that," and "I'm not like them," and "this is just never going to happen for me." Those negative thoughts will just run you into the ground.

When I feel like I can't control my thoughts there are a few different things I do, but one of them is simple. I slow down and close my eyes, then I picture a serene lake or river of some sort. And as the thoughts come into my mind I gently notice it and I picture each of these thoughts as a leaf falling onto the water and drifting by me. Then when another negative thought comes in, it floats to the water and down the stream. And I'll just do that over and over until I can consciously slow down my thoughts.

The other thing I do is for those times when I'm future-tripping or catastrophizing, playing a scene over and over in my head about something that hasn't even happened and probably won't ever happen. In those instances, I picture a huge red stop sign in my mind. It tells me to stop obsessing, overthinking, and going down this rabbit hole. I sometimes have to keep doing this, but it brings awareness to the mind and helps me remove myself from the cycle of negative thoughts. You can try this alongside visualizing what you want in your life so that you can create more positive space in your mind for what you're wanting to manifest.

Making "Hocus-Pocus" Real

Maybe this whole idea of manifestation sounds too simplistic, too out-there, or too good to be true, but a lot of powerful things are both simple and possible. Why do we feel that something so simple can't possibly work? All I can say is, it has been an incredibly effective tool for me to create the life of my dreams. What do you have to lose? See for yourself just how profound it can be.

PART III
Living Fully

CHAPTER 13

Ignore the Noise

How do you do it all? I get that question a lot. I've gotten pretty good at spinning a lot of plates at once, and that's a huge change for me because I used to feel overwhelmed every day of my life. The irony is, I'm doing so much more now than ever before, but I don't *feel* like it. When I'm living fully, I don't feel crippled by how much I have going on. That's because my life includes empty space too. Space to breathe, and to *be*. I used to cringe at that notion, and thought that people with empty space in their lives were just wasting time. Thank goodness we have the capacity to change.

One of the ways I've been able to do what people perceive as "a lot" in my life is recognizing the value in doing the minimum amount of work to achieve the maximum result. I find the shortest and simplest path to a goal, and I try not to let myself get pulled this way and that. I love how Warren Buffett put it: "You don't get any extra points for the fact that something's very hard to do. So you might as well just step over one-foot bars, instead of trying to jump over seven-foot bars."

That philosophy leaves a lot of room for living.

I know that sounds great and logical in theory, and maybe you've even read stacks of books or listened to a slew of podcasts about how to be superefficient with time-saving tips and methods for achieving the most in the least amount of time. And perhaps those strategies even work for you for a little while. They can make life feel easier. But then, the wheels come off the bus and before you know it, you're once again sweating and toiling on the hard road, wondering how on earth you're ever going to get to the bottom of your never-ending to-do list before you run out of time or energy. Sound familiar?

I'm not here to talk to you about the ins and outs of time management; I don't think it's as simple as that. I think it runs deeper. I want to get to the heart of the issue, the reason *why* we make things hard on ourselves in the first place. How we get away from what we know works in our lives and end up going on crazy, bumpy detours. Why do we go in a thousand different directions when we know exactly where we need to be headed?

One word: noise. We get distracted by the noise.

Here's a simple example. I know how to get in shape and stay healthy. Through the years I've almost become a professional at it. I know the exact fitness and eating plan that works for my body and it is foolproof. So why the heck do I try keto? Or paleo? Or vegan? Or any other popular diet everyone's talking about? Because I'm listening to the noise of fads and trends. I'm not doing what I already know works for me and instead, I'm choosing a more difficult path, one that isn't proven in my own life.

It's so crazy how we don't listen to what we already know. We forget so easily. It's one way noise can complicate our lives and make it much harder to get things done. But you have to really tune back in to yourself and what you know to be true and what has a proven track record in your own life. Then we are able to more effectively *ignore the outside noise* and walk a more efficient path. *That* is the secret that has allowed me to do everything I want to but still have the time to take it all in and appreciate the beauty of those ordinary, everyday joys of living.

But make no mistake, I fall out of this rhythm sometimes, and have to begin again the process of taking my life back. Because it really is just that. Taking my life back, not handing it over to the noise of self-doubt, the louder voices in my head, or just the incessant need for more. Recently, I was caught off guard by a season of stress and overwhelm. I was juggling a lot, as usual, but it felt different. The small tasks took over my mind and the larger ones caused me so much anxiety I couldn't focus to effectively do any of them. My family got the worst version of me: stressed and overwhelmed and empty. It was like there was a hole in my gas tank and instead of plugging up the hole I just kept pouring more gasoline in to keep moving forward. I thought I could outrun it if I just worked harder.

That is exactly the way my mind worked when I was in active addiction. In a recent session with my therapist—a person who has been an amazing asset in my journey through so many life phases—she told me that I had relapsed. *Relapsed? But I hadn't had one sip of alcohol or touched a substance, not even close.* She explained that it was an emotional relapse, and if I didn't change, it would ruin my life just as the substances and perfectionism had before. It didn't make sense at first, but the more I thought about it, and the more we discussed the noise I was listening to, the more I began to see that she was right.

Back in the days when substances were my drug of choice, I was listening to a lot of noise too. It's as plain as day to me now when I started listening to the noise of fear, or scarcity, or my own mind telling me that I could control everything . . . if I just worked a little harder. It is an old sound but it still plays in the background of my life even today. That's why I need to be so mindful about listening to my desires and tuning out the noise. We all do.

Noisy Nonsense

There are all different reasons that we listen to and give in to the noise and thus make our lives harder than they need to be. I used to do it because I was desperate to prove to others how much I was capable of accomplishing. I found value in those exhausting days of my past life that left me run-down and ragged. I took on too much in the name of proving my worth.

"*Sure, I'll emcee that live auction.*"

"*Yes, I'll do your hair and makeup.*"

"*Of course, I'll host that party!*"

I had not yet come to realize that saying yes to more than I knew I could handle would not enrich my life or help me get to where I wanted to go faster. I also didn't realize those things would take my focus off the life I really wanted to live. So, I said yes so much that I ended up resenting the people who asked me, my own family members, myself, and pretty much everyone else on the face of the earth, right down to the mailman.

Now I know that the people around me never saw my ability to do a million things as a badge of honor like I did anyway. I was wearing myself out for nothing. I wasn't tuned in to my true desires or what a full life actually looked like for me, and instead, I was responding to what I *thought* was expected of me. **That's a form of noise.** I wish I could go back and bang this book over my head a couple of times during that marathon I kept running on repeat. Is there similar noise in your life propelling you to take on too much, all so you can prove you're so capable?

The value of saying no, and knowing when to say no—that's a topic that gets a lot of airtime. But it also misses the mark a bit. We have to look at what's motivating us to say *yes* to the point of running ourselves into the ground. Why don't we carefully weigh and prioritize our yeses instead of handing them out to everyone like candy on Halloween? That's the question we need to be asking ourselves.

While the specific answer is different for everyone, it's usually because we are listening to noisy nonsense. Saying yes to a thousand other requests instead of saying yes to what we truly need and want in our lives will only make our days longer and harder than they need to be. If you can relate, ask yourself, what has driven you to spread yourself so thin that you can no longer experience fulfillment in your days? Find ways to silence that noise and listen, instead, to what's truly important to you.

Other People's Noise

We can also end up making our lives harder by listening to other people's noise, and it can become a giant roadblock if we let it. We already covered what it means to surround ourselves with people who light us up and help us find our inner fireworks when they've gone out. But let's spend a little time on the flip side now and think about those "noisy" people in our lives.

Think of the person or people in your life who cause you to feel not so great about yourself, or who stir up self-doubt or fears for you. They're the ones who don't celebrate your successes and try to one-up you instead. The family members who are so in their own stuff that they don't even realize they're casting a web of negativity. Or the people (online or in real life) who hurt you, purposely or not, with words that cut you and echo in the back of your mind.

There are two ways we can deal with these types of noisy people.

First, we can limit our exposure to them and increase the time we spend with people who inspire, motivate, and encourage us. Yes, it can be that simple. We can choose not to allow noisy people into our space. I think all too often we let them in because we feel in some way obligated to them, or maybe it's purely out of habit. But it's important that we play an active role in choosing who we spend time with and keeping those who don't make us feel as great a bit further outside our circle.

Second, if their presence is unavoidable—say, if they're a member of the family or someone we work with—then we can mentally and emotionally prepare ourselves before we spend time with them. The idea is to not give them the power to impact you negatively or drown out your thoughts with their static. Sometimes awareness is half the battle and just enough to help you not allow their noisy interference to get through. Or you can decide in advance how you will react to that person, and make a deal with yourself that no matter what is said, you will not allow it to get under your skin, and you will remain calm. You could even resolve to meet their negativity with sheer positivity. The truth is, noisy people are inevitable in life, but we do not have to give them any power to derail or distract us.

Here's what I want you to always remember though: their noise is just that—*their* noise. Whatever they have to say about you, your abilities, your goals, your dreams, your life is not for you or about you. They'll try to spin your wheels and create doubt and unnecessary hardship if you let them, but you don't need to take that detour.

The Noise of Busyness

Sometimes the noise in our lives is something we actually create in the form of busyness. How many "how are you?" text messages have you answered with "Oh my gosh, I am soooooo busy." That used to be my tagline. But it's a risky way to live life because it can have this hyperspeed effect where we start to lose time and wonder where the days, weeks, months, and eventually, years went. Running here and there, jamming as much as physically possible into every waking second—has that ever resulted in a feeling of bliss? Have you ever gone to bed at the end of a day like that and thought, I sure do love my life. I am relaxed, my soul is satisfied, and I am peaceful inside. I'm guessing not. Usually a day like that results in exhaustion, moodiness, and stress. So, what about a whole life like that?

I don't want you to think that living fully means filling our days with tasks; fully is not the same as full. Sometimes our days get filled up because we aren't being purposeful about how we manage our time and we aren't protecting certain hours for what matters most. This goes back to balance and making sure we prioritize our time. But sometimes we get busy doing little things because we're procrastinating the big ones.

When I purposely stop myself before I get to the frantic stage, and tune back in to myself and my immediate goals, I can rein in the busyness and get back to business. I have really honed these abilities during the process of writing this book, especially while being mom to my one- and two-year-old boys.

I have also become very aware of how easy it is to spend a whole day, week, or life responding to other people. I get thousands of emails, direct messages, private messages, text messages, and other forms of communication on a regular basis. And I love communicating with people in these ways; I really do. I feel blessed that people want to tell me or ask me something, and I will never take that for granted. But I have had to strike a balance between feeling connected with others in my life and spending my whole life in response mode.

Maybe you've also known what it feels like to be buried under a message mountain and worried about how to adequately respond without letting it take you over. Give yourself permission to not always respond, or at least not immediately. It can help you turn down that noise of busyness so you can focus your time on what matters most.

Fulfilling Others' Needs

As we take on more responsibility in our lives, we can easily let that running mental list of the needs of others become so loud in our heads that we can't even hear ourselves think. We might even let everyone else's preferences supersede our own to the point that every extra second of our life is filled up trying to cater to someone else. It's a catch-22 because we want to rise to the occasion and do well for those who need our time, but we don't want to lose ourselves in the process.

I'm not saying the answer is to be self-centered, or that we should ignore the needs of loved ones in our lives—of course not. Meeting the needs of others can be deeply fulfilling. This is true for me, especially as it relates to caring for my family. But I've found the key is to not create unnecessary busyness on top of the necessary busyness that comes along with the responsibilities of having a husband and children at home.

And with certain things, we might even convince ourselves that no one can do them as well as we can, so we shoulder even more responsibility than we actually have to. Have you ever found yourself thinking that way? Like you're the only person in the world who can do certain tasks exactly right so you refuse to ask for help? If left unchecked, this can lead to a martyr mentality, where we walk around feeling like we're doing everything all the time for everyone else while no one's looking out for us. We have to look out for ourselves, though.

Tuning Back In

Most of the time, we don't follow the noise on purpose—it's usually a habit we've formed. I want to make it easier for you to spot the habit. For instance, the next time you're about to say yes to yet another promise you shouldn't make or can't keep, ask yourself why that's your knee-jerk reaction. What is the specific noise you're listening to? Is it that you want someone else to think you're always reliable? Or that you have to somehow make up for a perceived failing in some area of your life? Once you've identified the underlying reason you were about to say yes, it should be much easier to confidently and politely decline. It can be as simple as "I don't want to spread myself too thin, but I'm flattered you asked me." And then . . . no guilt, no looking back.

What is the loudest noise in your life? In what ways do you listen to it and allow it to make your journey twice as long? How has noise caused you to put obstacles in your own way that didn't need to be there? Think about it. I want you to become aware of all the ways noise is impacting you.

I have become very intentional about my choices so that there is always space for what matters to me the most. I try very hard not to take on so much professionally that it impacts my ability to enjoy my life. And I don't get so focused on meeting other people's needs that I abandon my own needs completely. In making all my decisions, I always try to return to that inner voice that speaks to me. And I have to know the difference between my inner voice and the outside noise.

There is no prize for making things harder than they need

to be. Life doesn't award us extra credit for going down every rabbit hole or for making it over roadblocks we put up ourselves. We can end up handing over years of our lives and the possibility for all kinds of happiness simply because we're answering to some hollow noise instead of the song of our spirit.

CHAPTER 14

Quieting the Voice of Fear

"Relax," the nail tech said to me for the third time. My hands were so stiff that she could hardly file my nails. Her comment snapped me out of my deep thinking and hard stare into the distance. I realized I'd been bracing myself, like my world was going to implode at any moment. I pulled my hands back, gave them a good shake, and did my best to laugh it off.

"Oh, I'm relaxed," I lied. "It's just . . . you know . . . this is my first time being out of the house since having my son. I *never* leave him. I haven't in seven weeks. I know he's okay. It's his nap time anyway. But now as I sit here, I'm so nervous my milk is going to come in." The woman's eyes started to widen as I talked ninety miles a minute, barely pausing to take a breath. I carried on. "Actually, my pump is in the car. I'm breastfeeding, I'm basically a cow at this point. There's so much milk! I mean, I'm grateful there is. I have so many friends who have struggled to produce enough. They're drinking all kinds of teas and taking supplements. So, it could be worse. But when I start to feel it, I just know I better pump right away or else it gets everywhere."

The nail tech blinked slowly and said nothing, probably regretting telling me to relax in the first place. I'd lost control of my inner monologue as it spewed out into the open—harder to contain than my breast milk, I guess. For no logical reason at all, I was rapid-fire justifying myself to a stranger.

My justifying didn't stop there. I then proceeded to tell every woman within ten feet of me that my baby was with his dad, *not* a sitter, and that I was only going to be gone for an hour. I might as well have stood up on a chair and shouted, "I'm drowning in mom guilt, so I feel the need to ensure that everyone knows I have not abandoned my newborn son so that I could get a gel manicure."

I had no control over the words that came barreling out of my mouth like wild mustangs every time I made eye contact with another human being. New baby. Old fear. Old fear of what people would think of me. Fear that they were judging me, assessing me as a terrible mother. Fear that they didn't think I was doing something in my life as well as I could, or as well as I should, or as well as some other person was. Fear that I actually *wasn't* doing things well enough.

I fell back into silence, something I hadn't had a lot of lately, but I kept feeling this need, this undeniable yearning to explain myself. Every time the salon door opened, my eyes darted over. *Please don't be someone I know. Someone that knows I left my baby at home. Or someone who follows me online and knows I recently had a baby, yet here I am, enjoying the luxury of having my nails done.* I couldn't bear the idea of that possibility.

Mom guilt is something I never saw coming until its headlights were in my windshield. I don't think any new mom could possibly anticipate the depth and breadth to which we are capable of guilting ourselves over how we parent our children.

However, you don't have to have children and the subsequent mom guilt to know what I'm talking about. Think about any time in your life when you've second-guessed yourself, or when you've felt the need to justify yourself to anyone. That self-doubt usually comes from one place: underlying fear. I covered earlier all the flavors of fine. Well, there's also a buffet with all the flavors of fear: fear of failure . . . of pain . . . of causing our child pain . . . of judgment . . . of change . . . of regret. And we tend to devour them like we're on a two-week cruise, going back to the buffet for seconds and thirds. And that's true for all of us, whether we are parents or not, married or single, young or old. And you may not even know that you have a fear (or more) hidden within you at all. But fear can be quiet and sneaky.

Fear can be pervasive. Fear can be crippling. Fear can be the most powerful adversary to a full life.

No One's Immune

Before each season of *The Amazing Race*, the producers always interviewed the contestants, and one of the key questions was "What are you afraid of?" Of course, they wanted to know because it allowed them to introduce challenges that forced us to face at least one of our fears. When they asked me that question, it was funny because I realized I don't have any phobias. Heights? No problem. Spiders? Nope. Snakes? Definitely not. When I was a little girl, I'd catch snakes in our yard and bring them into the house to my mom, who was terrified not only of snakes but of what was going to become of her daughter with the odd snake obsession.

I had always been such a tomboy, completely undeterred by any kind of animal, reptile, insect, or physical challenge. And as a young person I was also a bit of a daredevil, constantly climbing up and jumping off things, to the point that I kind of freaked people out. But phobias are one thing. As you now know, I did have some deep-seated fears of another variety: how others perceive me. And the producers figured that out for themselves when they got the results of the extensive psychological tests they did on me as part of the interview process. They discovered that I'm very competitive, and thus, my biggest fear was losing. So, while one competitor might have feared the competition itself, I was terrified of not coming in first place, no matter what the challenge was.

These kinds of fears, the ones that have driven me at certain points of my life, exist only inside my head. I've thought many times that I had finally successfully tucked these things away—fear, guilt, and comparison—but I've come to see that they lie dormant in the DNA of my life. Only to flare up when I'm tired or stressed. Or, apparently, post-pregnancy hormonal. Can you relate? It's as if we're carriers of fear always, and no one is immune.

I took a poll amongst my followers to find out what they felt the biggest threat to living fully was for them. Every other answer of the thousands I received was fear. Literally half of everyone who responded had something to say about fear. I was floored, but I was also excited. Why? Because fear is internal, and therefore, it is something we can control. When dormant fears do get stirred up and activated, there are ways to get a handle on them so they don't hijack our lives. This was a pivotal realization for me, and it can be for you too. Because make no mistake—fear *can* steal a life.

The Case for Fighting Fear

There are no two ways about it: fear can grab our happiness by the neck and wrestle it to the ground. It can sneak in and redirect our consciousness from would-be precious, memorable moments and plunge us instead into the dark waters of our thoughts. How many times have you taken a mental detour from a perfectly wonderful reality into some foreboding or even terrifying thought? Like you've entered some other dimension? How often has a worry about what *could be* stolen the joy of what actually *is*?

As if that wasn't enough, slowly, decision by decision, fear can take us on a journey of living shrunken, scared lives. One in which we settle for an in-between state where we're not striving for the things we really want out of life. Fear, in fact, can cause us to choose a totally different life. Living fully is about choosing the best version of our life. But if you're chronically afraid, you can't choose your best life. Fear takes over your mind and blocks everything—happiness, creativity, confidence, ability—and it leads you down an alternate path. Fear kills from the inside out. Nothing good or bright or magnificent ever blossomed from a seed of fear.

And even if we know all of that to be true, still, we give in. Too often, we let fear win. We allow ourselves to make choices not out of what we want or need, but instead, out of what we are afraid of. Have you ever shied away from something because you were afraid, or stopped short of taking a risk because of the "what if" voice in the back of your mind? Have you taken the safe, known road because the very idea of the unknown was terrifying to you? Fear can keep us from reaching beyond our current circumstances, and it can stop us from taking chances or chasing our passions. Of course that will lead to us feeling less fulfilled; how could it not?

How often do we let the fear of change force us into complacency? We think, *Change is so hard, and how do I even know it'll be better on the other side?* That's not us talking, though. That's fear. Oh, it might sound exactly like our voice in our head, and we might think it's who we really are, but it's 100 percent fear acting on our behalf. We have to keep a watchful eye and ear out for those times when we think we're in charge but it's really fear acting as an imposter.

Anytime you find yourself looking for the path of least resistance, it could be fear lying to you and trying to make you believe you aren't capable. If you hear yourself think, *I could never do that*, or *I'm not any good at that*, or *I'm not cut out for it*, or really anything that even slightly resembles self-doubt, you are leaving invaluable life experiences on the table, all because you're listening to the voice of the imposter.

Fear is at the root of everything that holds us back, so getting it under control is essential.

A New Way of Wrangling Fear

Getting a handle on fear requires some work, and it means being willing to look inward and grab a hold of your thoughts before they become a runaway train. When we're living life outside the confines of fear, we are able to clearly hear and follow the voice that's calling us to something more. Because when we aren't wringing our hands and wasting our valuable brainpower on what might happen or the worst-case scenario or the endless what-ifs, we suddenly give our minds all this runway to do, create, envision, and manifest so much more for ourselves.

Here's where my take on the topic of fear diverges from the popular perspective. It was a landmark moment for me when I started looking at it this way. The goal is not to *conquer* fear. It is *not* to eradicate it and become fearless. Like I said, it will always be there; no one is immune. My goal, however, is to put it in its proper place.

I'm obsessed with systems; I have one for everything from laundry to my pantry to packing, and I also have a system for managing fear. It goes like this: Once I've identified a fear or anxiety, I determine whether it has value. Meaning, is there something I can learn from the fear? Is it prompting me to make some kind of change in my life? Is it trying to protect me? Because some fears do serve a purpose. And if it does, I react accordingly. I make a change to the way I'm doing things. And I prevent that fear from overwhelming me. Once I've gone through that process, the fear naturally quiets down because I've addressed it.

On the other hand, if a fear doesn't have any value, meaning there's no action required, then I put it where it belongs—in the back of my mind where it cannot cause any harm. It's still there, but it's quiet. Anytime a "halting fear" gets kicked to the front of my mind ("I could never do that" or "I can't"), I remind myself that it has no value to me. I recognize that it serves no purpose in my life, it does not better me in any way, it does not improve my life or fulfill me. It is like negative energy, or dark matter. I know that if I let it loose inside my brain that it will only waste precious time, steal my happiness, and wreck my focus. Sure, the fear is there, but it's not up-front in my mind trying to overshadow my thoughts. I picture it like a landscape. Fear is part of the landscape of my thinking, but it's in the background, not up close, dominating my every thought. Or I'll begin looking for ways to prove a halting fear right, and once I attach enough proof to it, it gives it wings to fly.

This system allows me to manage any kind of fear that rises within me. Because just ignoring it or shouting back some kind of cliché will only cause it to remain and allow it to get stronger and louder in my life.

Once you get better at recognizing fear, you will be able to feel it coming on. Then, before it turns into a halting thought like *I'm just not going to do the thing*, or a doubting motion like *I'm not good enough to do the thing*, you examine it. You look at it and ask, "Does this fear have value?" For instance, if you want to be a blogger but you're too scared, look at the fear. If that fear is saying, "I don't know if I'll have enough time to do this and keep my day job so I can pay the bills," then you have to assess it and respond accordingly. But if the fear is saying, "What if people judge me, make fun of me, or say I'm not good enough or outgoing or well-spoken enough," those are the fears that have no value and you can quiet them.

So many people want to wallow around in a pool of fear and they think all fear is created equal. But remember there are ones that can serve us and ones that can stop us. We can take action with the fears that can serve us, and with the halting kind, every time it rises, we can put it back in its place.

Quiet Is Key

I struggle with the fear of being judged but I've come to realize there is a gentle way of putting it in its place and thus *quieting* it. I know some people would say, "You need to have a thicker skin! Don't let that stuff bother you. Those people don't even know you." But when we decide to toughen up and to have a thick skin, we sacrifice connection with other humans. I don't want to suddenly and completely stop caring about what others feel when they interact with me or my presence online. To me, not caring is a form of detaching, disconnecting. I crave connection and I love people, even the ones that don't like me back. That's one of the qualities that has allowed me to exist in the space of social media—I genuinely feel that connection, and those who interact with me feel it too. So, instead of not caring at all, I consider the criticism. I hold it up, look at it, and see if there's anything for me to take from it.

For example, if someone says they can't stand my accent, I throw that comment away immediately. That's an easy one. But when someone says I shouldn't send my oldest son to preschool because I'm home all day and he should stay with me, that one stings. So, I look at it more closely, and then I compare it to reality: My son is thriving. He loves school for the few hours he's there a couple of days a week. Kyle and I are home with him all the time, and when he is at school, that gives us one-on-one time with his little brother. It works for us. My own thoughts are louder, true, and more important than someone's comment. So, I take fear of outside judgment, and I realize it does not apply. And the fear it had stirred up in me at first (*Oh no, am I making a mistake as a mom?*) is quieted. The fear is still there but it isn't louder than my own thoughts.

What are the thoughts you need to turn up the volume on and what are the fears you need to quiet?

Bring your awareness to the fact that you might be caught up in a loop of your own thoughts. Doing this lets the air out of the balloon, deflating the fear to a more reasonable size. Then you can put it in a drawer in your mind, out of sight. And you don't run the risk of making decisions as a result of that fear.

Faith over Fear

It's nearly impossible to be faithful and fearful at the same time. Giving in to the fear means putting aside your faith . . . your faith that things will work out, that you are on the right path, that you are capable, that God will protect you and deliver you from whatever trial you may face. This is another reason why I so often rely on my faith and my spiritual journey—because it counteracts fear's effects. When my system for managing fear doesn't feel like it's working, or when a fear cycle grabs hold and almost becomes an addiction, I return to faith.

Because fear is an undeniable reality, I'm not telling you to try and pretend it isn't real or to permanently sideline it, because that would just be a lie. But by knowing what we stand to lose if we allow it to permeate our lives, we can answer the urgent call to get a grip on our fear before it threatens our happiness. That's one of the most important decisions we can make on our quest for a fuller life.

Each time I hear that tiny voice of fear muttering in the background, I act quickly to quiet it so my spirit can speak louder. And as it does, I am reminded of my dreams and desires, my hopes and wishes, goals and aspirations, and the everyday pleasures of life.

CHAPTER 15

Sugar and Spice

I learned to exist in a big world at a small age. When I was just ten years old, I had already been making my way as a young musician around my home state for a while, and the events I was being invited to perform at were starting to get larger. One particular invitation was pretty big for any aspiring musician, but especially for a child, and that was when I was asked to sing the national anthem at an NBA playoff game—the Houston Rockets vs. the Utah Jazz at the Compaq Center in Houston, Texas.

Singing your nation's national anthem to thirty thousand people . . . at age ten? It felt like a dream to a small-town girl like me.

On the night I was to perform, before going out onto the court, I can remember clutching my Giga Pet. Now, in case you weren't raised in the same generation I was, a Giga Pet was a small key chain toy, a digital "pet" of sorts. And it required you to care for it by pushing certain buttons to "feed it" or "take it out." It's funny to look back and think of myself holding a little toy in such a monumental moment.

When it was time for me to get into position on the side of the court, I turned to my sister and carefully handed my Giga Pet to her so she could watch it while I performed. I was just a child, and this was a serious, grown-up thing—singing during a live televised event with people standing up for something that is so much more than a song. There was such a weight of responsibility, but at the time, I had no hesitation in carrying that weight.

When I saw my cue from the announcer, I walked to the center of the court. I could hear the sound of my dress shoes walking across the hardwood—click, click, click, click. Then the lights shut off everywhere in the entire arena except in two spots: the American flag, and where I was standing. I waited there in the dead silence, with the bright spotlight enveloping my little body, microphone in hand. You could've heard a pin drop. There are two places I've been in the world where the silence was deafening: on the top of a mountain, and when people rose for the national anthem in that arena. I guess you could say I experienced both of those on the same night.

Charles Barkley, Hakeem Olajuwon, Karl Malone, and other basketball icons were lined up about twenty feet in front of me, but for those two minutes, the court belonged to a tiny girl. And I sang my tiny heart out. *This*, I thought, *is what I was born to do*.

The news station that covered stories in the tristate area came to my school the following week. They interviewed kids in my class, my music teacher, my family. I still remember to this day what my music teacher shared in her interview. "When God sprinkled cinnamon and sugar on everyone's pieces of toast," she said, "He sprinkled a little extra cinnamon and sugar on hers." I've always kept that in my heart. Even during the times when I've felt like a plain old burnt piece of stale bread, I remember those words. But they're not just for me. We all have a little extra sugar and spice—it's what makes us unique—even if you haven't been told so by someone like my music teacher. Could you maybe use a reminder of your own extra sugar and spice?

Do You Accept Me?

A few years after that first performance at that NBA game, I was invited back. The first time, I'd been focused purely on how much fun it was and how cool it felt to be singing there. The second time, I was fifteen years old, and things were a little different. Somewhere between eleven and fifteen, the world starts to really sink its claws into us. I was more aware of others looking at me. Suddenly, it was really important what outfit I wore—a gold top and fitted bell-bottom pants, and much higher heels. I took my glasses off, and left my hair down instead of up in pin curls.

I was more nervous because I could *feel* eyes on me. This time, it wasn't simply about a song I wanted to share with the world, but it was also a bit of *Do you accept me?* What a difference those few years made. Society had, to some degree, gotten its hooks into me and fundamentally changed my perception of the exact same event. It was as if some of the sugar and spice was scraped off that piece of toast.

Is there a point in your life when suddenly you began to focus more on being accepted than just being yourself? And has it kept you from doing something you loved, or sharing some part of yourself with others?

The world, if we let it, can change our entire trajectory. That "Do you accept me?" mentality can become our guiding principle, moving us slowly away from who we truly are and the things we love to do.

I think that happens to a lot of people. The world asks,

sometimes demands, that we conform, and if something about us doesn't fit the box it has for us, then our instinct is often to throw it out so the world will accept us. But then we can only become concerned with being accepted for who we are on the outside. Or even a false perception of what we feel we need to display outwardly.

Sometimes it's not the world that will nudge you to scrape off your extra.

I know in the beginning I said this isn't a "you're worth it" book, but here is the "you're worth it" part of the book, because it was part of my story. For a lifetime everyone around me applauded me. They sat front row at my performances, made signs with my name on them, and shouted my name during local parades. I've heard stories from the night of Miss America about people walking out into the cornfields of the county I grew up in and hearing roaring screams coming from all directions. For miles and miles people cheered me on. They lifted me up, gave me every single opportunity one would ever need to live a happy, deeply fulfilling, successful life.

And that, my friends, haunted me as I fell short.

You see, it doesn't always look a certain way when people end up crashing and burning, like I did. I had everything I needed, and I still blew it. And for years I carried the weight of not having something bigger to blame for what caused me to crumble. And that made me feel worthless. No one ever *told* me I was worthless, but I felt even more so, because it was completely my fault. So, I started scraping off my uniqueness. Making myself a little more ordinary because, by God, if I wasn't able to shine with a setup like I had, then I probably didn't deserve to shine at all. Maybe you can identify with having a similar foundation in life, and now, because of your choices, you feel like you have to make yourself blend in. But I have to say this, for the ones who had it all. It is still okay for you to get to the place where your life comes apart, and you're just as worthy of a comeback.

Fighting for Your Sugar and Spice

I started this book by talking about dangerous attachments that can steal our lives right out from under us, but *de*tachments can pose an equal threat. When we've detached from our individuality, we've lost an important aspect of who we are. Even when the world says they'd prefer us to be a little less extra, we have to fight to stay connected with what makes us . . . us—our sugar and spice.

So, *how* do you do that? It starts by really knowing what you're fighting for. Sometimes we get so caught up in our rhythm of life that it's hard to see those qualities that make us different and unique. But there are several ways to identify your sugar and spice.

Finding Your Essence

I've always liked the word "essence." It feels like it's a word that describes us as the original version of ourselves. It's who we are at our core. The dictionary describes essence as "a property or group of properties of something without which it would not exist or be what it is." This is something I go back to all the time. It's who I am when I'm my most grounded and in the flow. Your essence is what makes you who you are; without it, as the definition states, you would not be. Another way to say it is "spirit."

It's easy to lose that connection with our essence. So, the question is—how can we reconnect with it? Or maybe even connect with it for the first time as an adult? One of the simplest methods for rediscovering your true essence is to focus on your passions. In other words, spend some time and energy on the things that you liked to do before the world suggested that you stop. Ask yourself—what have you spent time doing that made you feel like that's the thing you were *born* to do? Or something that made you feel deeply happy and content, no matter what else was happening in your life? *That's* your passion. Maybe you've got several. But I'm confident that all of us have at least one. It just requires taking a little time to discover, or rediscover.

Once you've identified your passion, the key is to find ways to weave it into your life. It's not something that you acknowledge and then put off until some indistinct point in the future. Instead, become intentional about spending time doing what you're passionate about, and when you do, you will quickly find that you feel reconnected with your essence. You will be more present in the moment, more plugged in, and more like you are living your life as your truest self. Simply let your passions be your guide back to who you truly are on the inside.

Accepting Recognition

When others take the time and energy to recognize our unique qualities or talents, we can choose to let that really sink in and remind us of the ways in which we are special. But that's sometimes harder than it sounds. Think for a moment about the last time someone paid you a compliment. What was your initial reaction? Was it to . . .

. . . dismiss it in some way? "Thanks, but it was nothing, really!"

. . . hand the credit off to someone else? "Thanks, but it was really (blank) who did all the heavy lifting."

. . . or maybe even say how you could've done it better?
"Thanks, but if only I'd done (blank). I just didn't have time."

Why do we have such a hard time believing it when someone points out our best attributes? You've got to stop at "Thanks" and not add the "but." Start owning your goodness, your abilities, and your creativity and accepting those moments of praise as a reminder that you've got something different in you.

It will always be easier to focus on negative thoughts or feedback; I can remember every negative thing anyone's ever said to me, so I get it. But if you can focus as intently on the positive and allow it to guide you, it's another way to stay connected to your sugar and spice.

COMPARING CAREFULLY

Let's talk about comparison. We all do it, so let's not pretend we don't. We just need to remember that comparing ourselves can go two ways: it can be stifling, or it can be inspiring. When we start looking at someone else's talents, gifts, or even their drive and then compare them to our own and wish ours were more like theirs, it can halt us dead on our journey. When we focus so much on someone else's path instead of our own, we begin to meander off ours and onto theirs. It distracts us, and since we're not equipped to be on their path, before we know it, we're way out of our lane and completely stalled out in theirs.

On the other hand, comparison used correctly can be advantageous. I often look at people I admire and find ways to work into my life a version of what they've got going on, but in my specific style. It's a matter of identifying things that others are doing that could also work for you, but without planting seeds of discontent. It's a constructive form of comparison that can help us all grow brighter. It's emulating without copying.

CLING TIGHTLY

In this life we really have two choices. We can choose to recognize and express our qualities, passions, gifts, and talents no matter what the world says, or we can choose to conform. We can stay firmly and bravely focused on our journey, or we can drift around, getting cast about feeling lost or invisible. The choice is ours to make.

Maybe you haven't made a conscious decision yet, and if not, then today's your day to realize this. Or maybe you have, but then as time went on, you forgot.

Choosing to express and cultivate our uniqueness is not a box we check once and move on. Like so many other choices in our quest to live fully, it is a daily decision.

The world will try its hardest to dull your vibrancy so that you don't stand out in the crowd, or to overshadow you so you feel small and insignificant. It will tell you that you are either not enough or too much, and it will do its best to move you toward average. It will tell you to scrape off that cinnamon and sugar and just be toast because the people around you would be more comfortable if you could be a little less.

And sometimes that will be tempting. It will feel easier, for sure, to give in, but only in the short term. Each time we cling tightly to who we are and refuse to let the world win, we get a little stronger and we make the world a much sweeter place in which we spend our days.

CHAPTER 16

Love Prevails

Up until now, we've been looking at living fully under normal circumstances. But what happens when your life's path is altered by something so shocking that the earth seems to crumble underneath your feet? When the awful question *Is this really happening to me?* reverberates inside your body until you finally acknowledge the answer is yes. How is it possible in those crushing moments to imagine life at all, much less a full one?

Real life, as opposed to a work of fiction, is unpredictable. We never know how a story is going to end. With fiction, even tragedies, we can mostly tell where the story is headed. And we can prepare, at least a little, for what is to come. That's not always the case in real life. Maybe you've had an experience like that. I have too. But there is one thing I now know for sure: in the end, love always prevails. Living fully means loving fully, even in the face of loss.

I'm going to share with you a story like that. It belongs to my sister Jade, and she has graciously allowed me to share the intimate details of it with you. I want to tell it because I know, without a doubt, that it holds the power to help someone take those first breaths after the unexpected and the unimaginable has occurred in their life. Maybe that's you, but if not, I hope you'll still have the courage to read these words and know that you might one day be instrumental in helping someone else.

Where love was concerned it was going to take a special, one-in-a-million kind of man to be the perfect match for my sister. Cue Gef. From day one, they were a match made in heaven and they didn't date long before they were married.

They were excited to start a family, and my family all knew they'd make amazing parents. But a year passed, and nothing. So, they began exploring other options, and even those options failed. But still, they believed they were meant to become parents.

It was the month they were supposed to start IVF when Jade started to get a feeling she hadn't felt before in this process. Maybe you've had this feeling, the feeling you get when maybe, just maybe, you aren't supposed to be doing something you have planned. Even something you think will help you get what you truly want. And although she'd taken things into her own hands after years of believing that God would deliver her plan naturally, she felt the urge to give back control to Him.

She didn't say anything, and instead, silently waited for some kind of confirmation. A couple of days later, Jade's friend, who had just returned home from Italy, called her.

"Jade, I don't know why, but I keep seeing images of God holding you. It's as clear as anything I've ever seen." With those words, Jade had her confirmation. She told Gef, and they decided to put off the IVF.

That same month, she got pregnant naturally.

After five months of pregnancy, shopping for baby clothes,

daydreaming about names, and planning the nursery, it was time for Jade's twenty-week appointment. The one where they do an extra-long ultrasound, checking the baby's weight, the measurements, the rate of growth, and finally, the organs.

Jade and Gef sat in the OB-GYN office waiting for the confirmation that their miracle baby was perfect, as they knew he or she would be, so they could go on their merry way. But as the doctor walked in, something different happened. The doctor grabbed my sister's hands and looked her right in the eyes and said, "Jade, we need to talk about something. This baby has a heart defect. And we think there's a host of other things too. We need to immediately get you in to see a pediatric cardiologist and begin making a plan." But Jade and Gef already had a plan. *This* was their plan. Jade says that was the moment she started grieving.

Their baby would need to have a minor surgery after birth, another at five or so months, and then a final surgery at around three to four years old. But there was good news—the odds of surviving were high. When Jade told us the news, we were feeling optimistic given the circumstances and hopeful that we'd see the light at the end of all this, being the faith-filled family that we are. As the weeks went on, we knew there would be a mountain to climb, we just didn't know how high it would be.

Looking back, I'm so thankful we didn't yet know.

Blaise's Story

At nearly forty weeks, Blaise Augustine Cherwak was born via cesarean section. (With his middle name, they honored the church where they had gotten engaged.) The doctors and nurses seemed to be holding their breath, but after a few minutes, it appeared that everything was going well with Blaise; in fact, he seemed to be doing so well that they thought he wouldn't need that first surgery. The miracles just kept coming!

On the day they were set to leave the hospital with their new baby boy, Jade and Gef were packing up when the doctor came by to check on Blaise one last time. He noticed that he was slightly jaundiced so the doctor decided to keep him there an extra day. Minutes later, completely out of the blue, Blaise started crashing in my sister's arms. That was the first of what would be many times that the doctors had to resuscitate him. His heart began failing, so plans changed once again. Blaise, in fact, did need the first surgery, and fast.

The next thirty-four days held so many gut-wrenching ups and downs. Blaise went on and off life support and had three surgeries, after each of which, the doctors proclaimed, "Oh, we've got it this time." Making matters even worse, Jade and Gef weren't even allowed to be in the hospital at the same time because of the restrictions during the COVID-19 pandemic, so they couldn't comfort each other through those agonizing life-or-death moments, or to celebrate the hopeful ones.

All along, everyone was always clinging to the notion that this miracle baby would survive; we were completely unwilling to even consider anything other than that. One night, I stood six feet from the front porch of Jade and Gef's home, wearing a mask and rubber gloves, dropping off groceries in a pandemic.

When Gef walked inside, my sister said to me, "I don't think I'll survive. If he doesn't make it, I just don't think I can go on." I knew what she meant. Standing there, a mother myself, the agony of losing a child seemed too much to bear. *But that wasn't going to happen.*

"That's not going to happen, Jade," I said with assurance.

Blaise had been on life support for much of the previous thirty-four days, and while it sustained his life during that time, Jade and Gef knew prolonged use of these machines would eventually threaten it. They knew that when a baby was on life support past a certain point, there could be damage to vital organs. And in Blaise's case, the doctors started seeing signs of damage, so they knew once he came off life support this time, there was no going back. He had to survive on his own.

It was a Monday when they started taking Blaise off the machines, and he seemed okay at first. But on Tuesday, there was a rapid decline.

That morning, I called my parents. "Have you talked to Jade?" my dad asked.

"No, why?"

"They called us all to the hospital," he said. And immediately I knew.

We raced to Vanderbilt Children's Hospital, which was only blocks away.

When we got to the floor of the pediatric ICU, we were directed to the waiting room, where the whole back wall was windows offering an unobstructed view of Nashville. Looking out those windows, I wondered, *How did God bring them here? How is this life event part of their story?*

I snapped out of my trance immediately when I heard my sister's voice at the entrance of the waiting room. I turned around, and when our eyes met, the look of hope was gone. "Are you ready?" she said.

Who's ever really ready?

We were guided down a long hallway to room 1, and when we walked in, there he was. And there we were, faced with the challenge of having to say hello and good-bye all at the same time. How do you fully welcome something into your life that you know in the same day you will lose? How do you fully greet a life knowing it's about to end? How do you embrace something you'll soon have to let go? Well, now that I'm on the other side, I know the answer. My sister always says now that you're given the grace you need for the moment. But you can't feel it or understand it until that moment comes. It's a supernatural gift that's granted to us in these moments.

This seven-pound baby, connected to more machines than I could count, was so tired from all the fighting. He would open his eyes and look around slowly. This precious baby boy was perfect. Though his physical body was not perfect, he was. And the body, well, it's just a shell anyway. It's just the exterior casing for our souls, and as much as every single person in this ICU tried to help his body, it appeared that God had a different plan.

I will never forget all the vivid details of what went on around us that day. My subconscious mind soaked it in like a sponge. My sister's silver crisscrossed sandals and shiny gray toenails. The sounds of the machines beeping and pumping. The way the doctors and nurses moved around in the hallways, checking on other kids, doing paperwork, getting coffee. So many simple, everyday things. How we shuffled back and forth from his room to the waiting room, taking turns throughout the afternoon because only two people could see him at a time.

Life was going on all around us, both in the hospital and in the world, as we were preparing for this sweet, innocent baby to leave this realm and pass on to the next. It all exists permanently in my memory.

Most of all, the memory that I will forever cherish is when I got to hold him. I whispered, "Hey, Blaise, I love you so much. I'm so happy I got to meet you." He gazed up at me. I can see his precious eyes even now as I write this.

Our immediate family poured in over the next several hours, and before long, we were all together there in the ICU waiting room. There were lots of conversations during that time—lots of tears, lots of hugging, moments when someone said something funny and everyone laughed and seemed to forget the pain for a minute. One moment like this involved a head of cabbage. Once we saw the direction things were going, I called Jade's OB-GYN and asked her if there was anything my sister could do to help stop her milk supply, which seemed to be the only thing that was going right in this time of bringing a baby into the world. She'd told me one way to do this is to put cabbage leaves in her bra, so I ran and got two heads of cabbage, and upon entering Blaise's room the next time, I brought the grocery sack in with me and set it on the end of the bed.

Instead of explaining the cabbage, I went straight into a conversation with my sister about Blaise, and timing, and feelings, and all the other things we'd been talking about that day. A few minutes later, "Oh, and by the way, the doctor said to put this cabbage in your bra and it will start to dry up your milk supply."

Gef immediately burst out laughing and said, "I was really wondering about that cabbage. I do love your papa's vegetables, but I thought this was an odd time for you to bring them to us." We all laughed about that for the longest time.

There were also excruciating moments, one of which stands out so much for me because it is so telling of who my brother-in-law is at his core. He said, "I feel like when you're born, you get a gallon of love and you can divide it between whoever is in your life. And when you have a baby, you wonder—how will I love this child enough? I don't have any more love to give. But then, you find out that you get an extra gallon with each child. I feel like I have this extra gallon of love and I can't give it to Blaise, so now I have it for Jade. I have two gallons of love for Jade, and I just feel so much more love for her." How about that? If you want to see a testament of faith and love, and the beauty that is life, then look no further than my sister and brother-in-law.

Any hopeful question we would ask—like "Is there a chance his heart could beat on its own when they turn the machines off?"—the doctors just looked at us and didn't say anything. We had still been hoping for a miracle, even when the doctors and nurses said they were sure that wasn't an option. They were so certain they could speak for God, I guess.

There are two times in my life that I've been on my knees in a bathroom. One was during the Miss America pageant, when I had rolled up my red formal gown while standing in a porta-potty, knelt down on the ground, and said a prayer. The other time was that day in the Vanderbilt Children's Hospital bathroom. Sometimes we say a prayer but it's more like yelling, asking, begging God for an answer. "How can you take a baby?" was my prayer in that moment. I just kept asking. "Why did you even give them this baby if you were going to take it back?"

When it came time to turn off the machines completely, my sister held her baby as she'd done for thirty-four days before, and it only took thirty seconds for his earthly body to finish. And just like that, he was gone.

The doctors allowed me to come back into the room a little while later. He looked so different not being connected to machines, lying there in his onesie. My sister asked if she could pick him up, as if she needed permission. I nodded. I remember this scene often. Almost every day. She looked like the pietà statue of the Virgin Mary with Jesus draped across her lap after He had died. God gave Mary her miracle baby and took him back too. And look what the world is now because of it.

Gef asked the nurse, "What do we do now?" For all this time, they had been doing nothing but preparing for this baby, getting ready to bring him home, and now what? The rest of the world was still revolving. But not theirs. The nurse sympathetically responded with the logistics of what would happen from here.

As we were all leaving the hospital, gathering up everything to be taken back home, there were three big plastic bags filled with stuffed animals. Giraffes, bunnies, elephants, teddy bears—all of their soft, furry faces smashed together against the inside of the bag. It struck me then, isn't that what grief looks like? So many emotions, all mashed together, suffocating, trying to get out.

At first, I was so worried that my sister would have a hard time being around my boys, Shepherd and Ford. We had dreamed so much about how Shepherd and Blaise would be best friends, and in the same grade at school. Now, I wondered if my boys would become a painful reminder of her loss. But I didn't have to worry long; they were the first thing she asked to see when she got home.

That night, the whole family was at their house. She was sitting next to me on the couch, and she just looked so bare. Before this, she'd always had eyelashes, hair, makeup, nails, but now, it was like she'd been stripped of everything. She started asking me if I thought Blaise was a baby angel or a grown-up angel. She said it was the first time she had thought about the details of heaven. She'd always believed in heaven, but said, "Now I have a child who lives there, and I just have to picture it." Within hours of losing her son, she was already searching for peace.

We had an intimate service where Jade and Gef gave the most amazing eulogy. They said they were determined to get through because they wanted people to know him. I sang a song called "Go On Without Me." I know that the only thing for us to do is to live our life to the fullest, because Blaise didn't get to. I know he was only a baby, but I can already feel that he doesn't want us stuck in our sorrow, mourning his memory for the rest of our lives. Instead, I think he would not want us to waste any time not living. "I don't want you to cry over my memories, so go on without me" is how the song ends. But the truth is, he's with us, little Blaise, bright as the sun, forever warming us with his spirit and thus renewing ours. He taught me that love prevails.

Our family went on from that unimaginable day to today.

As I write these words, it has been over a year since he left us. Jade lives more intentionally now than she used to. All of us do. And I can end this story with happy news, as my sister delivered a healthy baby boy named George in July.

LOVING FULLY

We've all heard the saying "It's better to have loved and lost than never to have loved at all." But do we live by that? Do we always take the risk that comes with loving with our whole heart, or do we protect ourselves just a bit? Have you ever stood back and looked at how much of yourself you're keeping behind a fence, or maybe even a cement wall, for fear of being hurt? How much do we hold our hearts back from experiencing the full joy of another person for fear of loss or rejection? There's that fear of pain again, keeping us from accessing our fullest life. I know it might make you feel powerful to hold back in some ways. It might make you feel like you're protected or in control. But all it really does is make each of your days a little less vibrant. Less meaningful. Just . . . less. You are meant to live life out there in the sunshine or in the rain, not inside a fortress of your own making. Loving fully is fundamental to living fully, and it requires a certain amount of vulnerability and faith.

Maybe you've experienced excruciating loss—whether it's in the form of divorce, job loss, or death—and you've decided you could never weather another storm like that, so you're just going to retreat from the risk. It's too much to bear, so you're going to play it safe, lock up your broken heart, so that it cannot shatter once and for all.

If you could, though, just for a moment, set your logical, protective mind aside and allow me to speak to the you beneath that: You're not meant to play it safe. You are meant for more. And so, you must decide—will you try again? Will you live, really live, again, outside the protection of the safe cocoon that you've built? It all starts by choosing to emerge and opening your heart just a little so love can do what love does. . . . Giving love and being loved are worth it.

If you have been through something that has changed you, I encourage you to find the beauty within those changes. I know it's hard to do this alone, and the good news is, you don't have to. When we can't guide ourselves to strive beyond our current reality, there are people, stories, or hardships that can be an external lighthouse to our new destination.

Blaise is my lighthouse, and I hope his story can be a bit of that for you as well.

CHAPTER 17

Curveballs

Up until my late twenties, I had never been broken up with. Ever. It was a thing I prided myself on—the ringless upper hand, always mine to pull the strings and conduct my own life's orchestra. The confident feeling of "I've got this; nothing will take me by surprise" allowed me to relax in relationships until I was ready for another. Like a dang pack of gum. Until I started losing grips with myself and inching further and further from my confident nature, my true nature. That's when the tables turned and suddenly, everyone started breaking up with me. Every single one of them.

During and right after my experiences on *The Amazing Race*, I was dating a guy that was much more put together than I was. He was in his final year of medical school and living in the town where he grew up. His family had literally shaped the community for ages. In theory, I was the perfect fit for their kind. Except I wasn't. I had a lot of loose ends. I was sort of drifting, with no clear goal, plan, or destination in mind. Sure, I had a lot to be proud of, plenty of noteworthy accomplishments from my recent past, but in that very moment, my life had come to a dead halt.

It was into our second year together that something started to feel off. We were dating long-distance, so things sometimes got lost in translation, but it seemed to be more than that. That's when I went to visit him.

I remember it so clearly; I had been there for a day or so, and we were sitting in his living room. Something between us felt different than when we'd first gotten together, like something was being left unsaid. I was holding my breath practically the whole time, and I kept getting that weird feeling that things weren't right. So, like I'd done so many times in my life, I decided to scratch the surface to hear something I wanted to hear. Trying to rustle up a response, some kind of reassurance, simply so I could feel better, I said, "What do you want to do? Break up?" What I had in my mind was this vision of him laughing out loud and calling me crazy. Never in a million years did I expect him to say yes.

Without so much as a pause or a heavy sigh, he quickly replied, "Yes. Actually, I do."

I was stunned. Speechless. I had opened the door and he had walked right through it. You probably know the feeling of what happened next. The dry mouth, the punch to the gut, the stillness but the racing mind, the rejection. He doesn't want me. Humans rejecting humans is the worst.

He gathered his keys (he conveniently had class fifteen minutes later) and left me sitting there, in shock, and on his turf. I vividly remember wandering out into the backyard where I called my dad. In a shaky voice, I said, "I think we're going to break up. I don't know what to do." I was by myself in the home of the man who had just rejected me then left me there, and I didn't have any idea what to do next.

I had been so immersed in that relationship that when I looked around, everything in my 360-degree view was him. Everything. I had completely abandoned myself. So when the proverbial umbilical cord was cut, I was breathing on my own as if for the first time, and all the blood sustaining my life was my own. It was as if I was standing in my body for the first time in a long time. He had been my life source. *Can I breathe? Is my heart going to work?*

"Get out of there," my dad said. He booked me on the only flight out of town, but it wasn't until the following day. *What in heaven's name am I going to do tonight?* I wondered.

My now former boyfriend drove me to a pink hotel on King Street in Charleston. He walked me to the room, and as I was about to close the door, I looked at him one last time, waiting for the change of heart. I still wanted to reconnect the umbilical cord. He shut the door. And I never saw him again in my life.

Wrapped up in blankets in my dark room that night, I felt like I was dying. Human beings can be fragile in the way we feel about ourselves, and it takes our whole lives to love and accept who we are sometimes. So, when someone says, "I don't want you . . . I want to disconnect my life from yours and never see you again," well, no wonder we don't speak and we sleep in dark rooms and we cry rivers of tears. When someone *else* rejects us, oftentimes it proves what we already believed. *I knew it—I was right all along. Of course he doesn't want to be with me.*

When the Bottom Falls Out

I flew home crying on the airplane with ten rosaries wrapped around my wrists, and I slept in my dark room for days. I thought the only good thing that would ever possibly come from this was weight loss. Ha ha. Our minds. But it wasn't the only good thing, far from it. I would not have ended that relationship myself, so fate did it for me. Back at home, everything felt so foreign to me. I quickly realized I didn't know how to exist in my own world anymore. When we have our lives so entangled with someone else's, we can get locked together like fabric. Maybe the other person can easily rip the seams out, but we're just a bunch of strings left hanging there. Unraveled.

Now I can see that I had been so detached emotionally from the reality of my life, existing so in my own head, completely immersed in this falsely idealistic world I'd created, that I forgot to check into the real life right in front of me. I was too busy planning for my future with him and telling other people about it to realize I was just spinning my wheels. I had completely set myself up to be blindsided by this curveball. That's how it happens. That's how it *always* happens.

And when it does happen, we are caught off guard. We often think it is the absolute bottom, the lowest, the worst, most life-altering moment in life. We think it's all over and we'll never be the same.

How do we stand on our own two feet when our life feels altered in such a deep way? How do we accept ourselves back again when another person hands us our heart? Or when it feels like all of life's doors just closed in our face?

Well, we just do. Eventually. Because with time, the pain always passes. It's always one step forward and then another. Until we're walking on our own again.

These kinds of curveballs are brutal at the time, but we eventually discover that, in truth, they were exactly what we needed, and we may even feel grateful for them. We look back and think, *Thank God it didn't work out. It was everything to me then. And now, it's nothing at all.* If we can find a way to know *this is only temporary*, we can then take a step in a better direction, right out the door of our own version of that pink hotel in Charleston. And furthermore, we can consider ourselves lucky that we were spared from having to spend one more day of our lives on that wrong path. Sometimes what feels like rejection is really just redirection.

We can choose to grow from experiences like these instead of getting stuck in them. I believe they are always guiding us to the life we were meant to occupy, with the people that will be part of our destiny. Sounds hippy-dippy, right? But it's true. Just like how our pain can be the catalyst for strengthening our character, our darkest moments can lead to our life's purpose. Mine sure did.

A Quicker Bounce Back

These curveballs can come at us in any area of life. We're going along, making plans, doing our thing, and then out of nowhere—bam. Curveball. It can involve your family, your business, or even your long-term life plan. It could be something minor, or something really, really serious. A spouse has an affair. You get laid off from your job. The doctor gives a frightening diagnosis. You don't get into the school of your dreams. If you've existed on earth for longer than five minutes, you know that life sometimes hands us tough breaks. But it's these unexpected ones that can cause us to lose our footing, especially when we've put all our eggs in one basket like I had.

It took me a long time to get over that breakup, and at the time, I had no idea why. I couldn't wrap my mind around what happened, or how things had gone so terribly and unexpectedly wrong. But over the years of one curveball after another, I realized my window of recovery has gotten shorter and shorter each time. Why?

When I look back to the first curveball and others like it, versus the ones I've experienced later in life, I can see what made them different. I was different. Before, I would just hold my breath and wait for the next perfect pitch to come along to get me back on level ground. But at some point, I realized that the pitch is completely *out of* my control, so what was I waiting for? I didn't need to wait around for the next relationship in order to get over the last one. I knew that regardless of what was thrown at me, I could handle it.

That brought my focus back to myself, which *is in* my control. And that was how I transitioned from barely making it through each time my life fell apart to, instead, building a stronger one from the rubble. I'm not saying it's always easy, but it is doable. We are fully capable of shortening that window of recovery after a curveball comes our way.

Remembering that we *can* handle curveballs is key. When these things happen and it feels like they send us into the stratosphere, we tend to forget a lot. We forget our values, how we deal with adversity, and we can even forget who we were before this thing happened. In order to move forward into a new, brighter tomorrow, we have to first *remember*. Remember who you are—most importantly, your values, what you believe, and what's important to you. I love how Brené Brown puts it in her book *Daring Greatly:* "What we know matters but who we are matters more."* I think that's never truer than when we are dealing with an unexpected blow.

The real danger comes when you make lasting decisions as the person who just got broken up with, or the person who just lost their job, or the person that was just handed a problem. The original is altered. Like a Xerox copy. Everyone knows when you make a copy of an image, a little something gets lost in translation. The image is just a little blurrier. If you make a copy of that copy, the image is now twice removed from the original. And it's a little blurrier. When we're in the middle of reeling from an unexpected event, we tend to take on that most recent version of ourselves. Our original is al-

* Brené Brown, *Daring Greatly* (New York: Avery, 2015), p. 16.

tered. It's like we walk around wearing a cloak of rejection, loss, or disappointment. But if we make our next move from *that* place, rather than as who we are at our core, our *original*, we set ourselves up for more problems. Another copy, more inconsistency from the original. It can become a domino effect. And worse, it can easily become a pattern, where every time a curveball comes, we make our very next decision from *that* place instead of from our authentic selves. Then suddenly we're five, ten, fifteen decisions down the road and our life is unrecognizable.

So, the way to get your feet back on the ground in these circumstances is to first reconnect with your values so you can then make decisions as *your more authentic self*. It requires a certain amount of discipline to set aside the emotions of the situation long enough to say, "Here's what is important to me. Here are the things I value above all else. Now, coming from those values, what is the next step that feels right and true to who I am?"

I have a friend who had to do this recently when she discovered a potential health hazard that meant she and her family would have to move out of a home they'd only just settled into. Overwhelmed at the prospect of having to endure another move with a young child, she felt paralyzed. She told me she didn't know what mattered to her anymore, and she was tempted to put her head in the sand and stay put. But when I asked her what is most important to her, what she values most in the world, she immediately replied, "My family." She answered her own question. The health, safety, and security of her family far outweighed the cost and inconvenience of another move.

From that moment on, she felt strengthened, courageous, and energized. She tackled the problem head-on, and in less than two months from our initial conversation, she and her family were out of their house and into a new one. It's amazing what we are capable of when we take time, assess, and choose to be driven by our values when we are taking on life's challenges.

When I received that devastating breakup blow, I was not able to move forward right away. I didn't know what to do. I mean, I had to call my dad, who made the decision for me and got me on a plane home. As I've grown, I have realized I can't rely on other people to make decisions for me even when I'm paralyzed. I have to make my own decisions as myself, not as the person who just had the rug pulled out from under her. Now, when the curveball comes and my mind is racing, instead of calling someone to ask what to do, I can slow down, remember my values, and then make the decision.

Of course, there's a fine line between support and reliance. We want someone to support us once we already know what we plan to do next. But we don't want someone to influence us to make a decision that we haven't even thought through simply because we don't want to face it, or we think we're too overwhelmed.

There's usually a lesson within the curveball—something we can learn about ourselves, about others, or about the world around us. And if we let someone else navigate us out, then we risk the lesson. If we ask someone what to do, nine times out of ten, they'll tell us what they think. But when we don't make our own decision based on what we really value, and who we really are, then we might put ourselves in the way of the curveball again because we didn't learn anything. It can become an ugly cycle.

The Gift of a New Direction

Every single curveball or form of rejection, *anything* I've been thrown, has *always* guided me to somewhere I needed to go. Every single time. It pushes me in a direction I wouldn't have known to go otherwise. It might be a battle getting there, but I always end up in a better place. So, when things don't go according to plan, I have to stop and remember that.

I have to remember that I may not know the answer, but I know there *is* an answer. Once I did recover from that first bad breakup, I went on to date a lawyer, an MLB pitcher, a golfer, a famous country music singer, and about five guys I met at random bars. And I thank the Lord that none of them wanted to spend their life with me, because ultimately, each one guided me in a new, better direction: toward Kyle. I had no idea at the time where I'd end up, or who I'd be with, but I knew that eventually it would all make sense. And now it does. My husband is everything I ever needed, and our relationship is nothing short of a home run.

Sometimes curveballs don't redirect us toward a new physical path in life, but instead, toward a new mental path. They might come about because we need to redevelop something about ourselves or our beliefs. Maybe we've been holding on to an old version of ourselves. Or we have unrealistic expectations about how our spouses or children should behave. Maybe we've been living up to someone else's ideal about parenting, working, or contributing to our community. Whatever they are, those old ideas may not be serving us anymore. At one point they used to make sense, but in our current reality and circumstances, they're no longer true or applicable.

The next time you receive a wild pitch, think about whether you need to revisit the way you've been thinking about yourself, your role, or others in your life. It might be time for some redirecting of thoughts.

What About Foul Balls?

Sometimes we flat out make the wrong choices in life. We choose the wrong people, careers, battles and we put ourselves right into the path of the curveball. For these moments, we need to extend ourselves some grace for making the wrong decision. With everything we already have to fight off and fight for in this life, the last thing we need to do is spend time beating ourselves up for choices we've made or regrets we're carrying around like deadweight. Yet, we often do it day after day, year after year.

Endlessly blaming ourselves for our mistakes or missteps has no place in our journey. Having grace for ourselves does. Don't dwell on the decision that got you into trouble; forgive yourself, learn from it, and get your footing in the new direction you're heading now.

I have now gotten to a point in my own life where I can honestly say that when some form of adversity comes my way, even in the middle of that adversity, I can say, "Thank you for what this is teaching me, and for where I'm being guided." Granted, there are times when I say it through gritted teeth, or in a tone that is not super thankful. But I do mean it because I know that it is through these things that I have found the gift of a full life.

When I interviewed Gabby Bernstein on my podcast, we discussed handling curveballs by focusing on what's thriving instead of what's falling apart. And how when we choose to focus on the positive, we can feel gratitude instead of despair. It was at the height of the pandemic, and so many people were caught up in the horror stories of 2020. We talked about how many people were showing great resiliency, courage, and humanity, and how much innovation and collaboration came about as a result of one of the most dramatic curveballs of our lifetime.

By shifting our focus to what's going right, we don't get so stuck on what has gone wrong. And then we can be open to receiving guidance for what is the next right step after any obstacle.

Any time we get knocked off our normal, stagnant, baseline existence, it's an opportunity to reclaim our lives. You don't want to get to the end of your life and wonder, *Is this it? Did I do okay? Did I take the risks and did I grow? And did I become the person that I always wanted to be?* Without these curveballs that feel so catastrophic when they hit, we could very well end up living in that "fine" state of mind, and leaving a heck of a lot of life unlived.

This is your one life. Do not leave it unlived; instead, aim to hit it out of the park, curveballs and all.

CHAPTER 18

Defy Gravity

The end of this book is your new beginning. It is your chance to take what you've discovered within these pages and finally grab ahold of the kind of life you want to live. I'm living proof of a life that could have gone one way or stayed exactly where it was. But it didn't. Because I chose a bigger life. I wrote this book hoping you will too.

I also wrote it to inspire you to choose that bigger life even as you hear your old life constantly calling your name in the distance. And yes, that will happen. Your old life will, at times, seem easier, more comfortable, safer, and familiar, and it may even feel like it's your true home. But it's not. You don't belong there anymore.

It's Your Turn

What will it take for you to finally step into your dreams? I've often noticed it seems like so many people are sitting around in life's waiting room. Pacing. Idly scrolling through their phone. Staring off into the distance. Waiting for someone to burst in and say, "It's your turn. Go right on in. Your *real* life, the life you've dreamed of, is on the other side of this door." Until that door swings open, they wait. And wait. And wait . . .

Have you been in that waiting room, living your life on pause? Are you *still* in that waiting room, waiting for your turn? If so, I urgently want you to realize something. Ain't nobody coming in the door to invite you to live your fullest life. Your name has already been called; you've already been invited. But I can't accept it on your behalf. That decision is yours alone.

Who you were and what you believed about yourself yesterday can be the first stage of a metamorphosis. But if you haven't started rewriting your story, and you're still caught up in an old story line, let me be very clear—in order to live a big life, you do not have to be born under some lucky star. We *all* have access to a bigger life.

The Backslide

If you think about how many motivational books you've read in your desire to seek a different life for yourself, only to then slowly morph back into the exact same version you were before, I hope I helped you find ways to make real moves this time. But it requires that you defy gravity, the gravity that tries to pull you back again and again.

I want you to know, without a doubt, your old life will relentlessly try to pull you back. That's the gravity you're going to defy. It's this invisible yet incredibly powerful force that you won't even notice is tugging you back to the ground again. This force is part of how we're wired. It's our brain's constant search for baseline, for normalcy, and for routine. So, you must be aware of this, expect it, and then *rage* against the constant temptation of an "easy" life.

We are the most vulnerable to gravity's pull when we are in neutral. When we're standing still. That's when we can most easily be overtaken. One little compromise after another, and before long, our lives are empty, devoid of meaning, and we are lost. This time, you must fight. This isn't your wake-up call; this is your stay awake call. You must not allow your life to slip back into neutral, where you are exposed and defenseless. If you fight it, if you *defy gravity*, it will become weaker as you grow stronger.

I learned some of this while walking around in the blur of addiction, attachments, and the haze of very real discontent. Squandering gifts I was given and dulling pain that I brought on myself over and over. But I learned the rest of this while in a state that we've all been in before: autopilot. Okay-ish, content mostly, fulfilled sometimes, happy as long as others around me weren't sad. And that state is the sneakiest of life stealers. And the hardest to stand up to and push back against, because it is so widely accepted. It is what the world accepts. But please don't accept it. "Good enough" is not nearly good enough.

Never in my life did I think I would go on a crusade to rock the boat of people doing "just fine" across the world. But when it happened to me, as I myself slipped backward into a so-so version of a life I had just fought for, I realized this was a dangerous place to be, and a place I never wanted to get drawn back to again. And I didn't want anyone else to get drawn in either.

Because when we slip back into our old ways, forgetting about the breakthroughs we've had, our lives remain the same. We kill the seeds of change that were trying to take root. And as we lose momentum, we place the book that struck a nerve in us on the shelf, out of sight, and we turn back to the familiar direction our lives were already headed. I hear it all the time. I'm sure you do too. It's because we value the comfort of our current situation over the discomfort that comes with making changes.

I feel as if often, people don't really want a bigger life more than they want the comfort of the familiar one they're already living. You must want this *more*. Even if it's just a little bit more, it must be your dominant thought. Then you must follow and bolster that thought with the new behaviors you've learned when you need them most. Old habits die hard, but true commitment does too. When you're truly committed to a new kind of life, you will create it.

When I was taking my first tricky steps onto a new path after treatment, I heard loud and clear the voices of everyone around me who thought I should play it a little safer this time around. They thought it was the title and the attention and the TV shows that had sent me on that wild path of destruction that nearly destroyed my life. So, they wanted me to lie low, stay under the radar, and take slow, cautious steps on my new path.

I can still remember my first brush with an opportunity that seemed a little too big after I got out of treatment. At that time, blogging was really popular and I decided that I wanted to start a blog. I saw it as an opportunity to express my creativity and encourage people. When I told my mom, she said, "Mal, I just don't know. I think maybe you should just get a job at a department store makeup counter. Wouldn't that be fun? You love makeup." The risk-taking, fearless, over-the-top spirit inside of me felt deflated at the thought. That's the perfect job for someone else, but it simply was not what I was being called to. I can appreciate my mom's line of thinking. She was afraid that blogging would put me right back into the limelight and a pattern of approval-seeking. She was looking out for me, thinking that taking fewer risks would be a safer path. She didn't want life to become too much for me again.

But for me, the reason I'd gotten pulled into the darkness in the first place was because I had been numbing out my vibrancy on repeat due to negative influences and perfectionistic obsessions. So, I was not about to let the well-intentioned, positive ones do the same. A cautious life was not the answer for me. Of course, there were times in the midst of creating that bigger life for myself that it felt bumpy, hard, and tiring, and I started to doubt it all. I felt that desire to retreat to easier methods. I could have chosen the easy road, but I didn't. I kept choosing the harder one that a lot of people were scared for me to take, and I never looked back.

Five years later, I host a top-rated podcast where I get to interview fascinating people, I've landed partnership campaigns with some of the top lifestyle companies in the world, I have a booming merchandise line, and I've written this book you're reading. I tell you this not so you'll marvel at what I've done. I share this so you can see how the harder, more uncomfortable road can be paved with gold. And not just the kind that fills your bank account, but the kind of gold that fills your soul.

All of your life experiences have been leading you to this exact point in time, and to this exact place where you are. Every single thing that has happened to you, every single choice you've made, everything you've thought was a mistake or a misstep, every decision that you regretted, every person who has impacted you negatively or positively, every dark corridor you've had to walk down or bright spot you've stood in—it has *all* led you here. That time was not wasted. *That's merely information for reformation*. What you do next is what counts the most.

If you're feeling fear around the edges, just know this: If you decide to go at this halfway, or to wait and see how you feel in a few days, or if you decide that you are, in fact, unable to do this because you're too busy, too tired, too overwhelmed with life . . . then here's what you actually need to be afraid of:

You need to be afraid of losing your shot at a fulfilling life. Because that is the actual sacrifice you are making if you give in to your fears. Don't risk it all simply because it seems easier to give in to the voice of fear.

A QUESTION . . .

Here we are. Now that I've shared with you many of the choices I've made throughout my life, I am handing you the microphone and asking you this question: Will *you* choose to live fully?

This is a serious question, possibly the most important one you've ever been asked. The pressure is on. What's going through your mind? Do you wonder if you're brave enough to face what you must in order to experience fulfillment?

Or are you ready? Do you feel like you *finally* get it and are ready to move beyond? Have you seen the light that you were blinded to before? Does it feel like you see now that you have to *fight* for this, and it's worth that fight? Is your heart welling up because you know—you *really* know—that you can and will fight against the lesser life that you've accepted in the past?

You are reading these final paragraphs in this book for a reason. Whoever you are, wherever you are, and however you've lived your life until this point, there is a real and true and valid reason for why you are reading these words. This isn't an accident. It wasn't happenstance that brought you this far. No. You got to this point. Where will you go next?

Take your life in any direction you want from here. Seek and find the joy in the journey, the pleasure in the pursuit, and the victory in the voyage. You can start today. Maybe you're going to resist the urge to settle for "fine" in your life, resolve to quiet the voice of fear, or get serious about discovering what balance looks like for you. It could mean reactivating your faith, or turning down the unnecessary and unproductive noise in your life. You might work toward uncovering hidden joys or defining your very own living legacy. Whatever it is, spread out your arms and live a deeply fulfilling and joyful life.

Living fully is the gift that keeps on giving *if* we keep on giving it to ourselves. Never stop. Until the very last beat of your heart, keep giving yourself that gift. This moment represents your chance to take what you've discovered in these pages and finally grab ahold of the kind of life you want to live.

Now, go live fully.

ACKNOWLEDGMENTS

Writing this book was the hardest thing I've ever done. I had breakdowns and breakthroughs. There were times where I felt I was on top of the world being divinely led, and times where I wondered if I could finish what I started. Through this process I toiled . . . and for one big reason: for the reader. I didn't write this book for fun or to check something off my bucket list. I wrote it to hopefully change some people's lives as mine was changed, and for this reason, I felt I was climbing Mt. Everest the whole time.

These people are the reason I've made it to the acknowledgments portion of the book alive. They were like Sherpas for me on my climb.

First and foremost, to Shannon Marven. There are almost no words I can find to express my gratitude to you. You are the single biggest reason this book exists. You have been so much more than a literary agent for me. You pulled this book out of me from the first day we met at that coffee shop years ago and stuck with me through passing bottles of breast milk to our driver so he could put them in the refrigerator between publisher meetings in New York City. You live permanently in my corner. You went through loss with me, triumph with me, and plain ole "I can't do this anymore" with me. You just have a way to help me find my spirit and my voice again. "Thank you" will never be enough. Also thank you to Rebecca Silensky Echols and the entire team at Dupree Miller. And to Lisa for being my book doula and helping me through this process with such grace and kindness.

To Becky Nesbitt and the entire Penguin Random House team, thank you for taking a big chance on a first-time author. Becky, your patience, encouragement, and constant attention to detail far exceeded what an editor's typical role would be. The day you spent the entire day in my home office with my children running around in diapers and staying so late we had to order Tazikis I looked at Kyle and said, "Dang, I'm lucky to have Becky Nesbitt." Thank you for believing in my message and making me feel like your most important project constantly although I know you had a lot of those. To be able to write my first book with the largest publisher in the world and a publisher like Tina Constable has been nothing short of a dream. Thank you to Campbell and Jess also for your enthusiasm and marketing expertise.

To Kyle, you are my greatest cheerleader and an *amazing* husband and dad. You sacrificed your career to help build mine and raise our babies during this busy season. You woke up with them in the middle of the night and took care of them on days I had to write. You never cease to remind me of the reasons I'm doing what I'm doing and why it matters. I adore you and the life we've built together.

To my little boys, Ford and Shepherd. I met Shannon the first time to talk about this book the day I found out I was pregnant with Ford, so it's safe to say these boys and this book have grown alongside one another from day one. You are the reason I want to do more than just coast through life. You are the reason I want to do it all big. You are the reason I want to live fully. You two have brought me unlimited purpose and constant joy. You are the greatest blessings of my life.

To my dad, Gary. Your constant pursuit of a full life is probably what planted a seed in me as a child to do the same. I am so grateful for our many adventures around the world together, for an example of humility amid success and the greatest PawPaw in the world. Thank you for never batting an eye at the wild things I wanted to do with my life and supporting every step of my journey.

To my mom, Lisa. Thank you for sacrificing all your dreams for the one dream of raising us. You gave us everything and more to begin our lives with joy and magic. You're the best Grammy and prayer warrior.

To my siblings Jade, Luke, and Gabriel. Thanks for being there through it all. The most fun, full moments of my life have been spent laughing with y'all (and your spouses, Gef, Caylee, and Jessica). I feel so lucky to be y'all's sister.

To my huge family, every aunt, uncle, and cousin, thank y'all for supporting and cheering for all my dreams and making for a rich life from the very start.

To my grandparents Bud and Marylyn Ervin, the ones I dedicated my book to because I've never known better examples of a full and vibrant life. You made me feel so special from the day I was born.

To my friends, especially Alex and Shawn, for talking me off a lot of ledges and being a constant source of laughter and fun.

To the people who help me in my day-to-day life, you know who you are and I could not have done this or anything without you.

To my hometown community of Union County, Kentucky. Thanks for making me feel like a star and rooting for me in every endeavor. Being from a small town like this is ingrained in everything I do and growing up around good people like you is a treasure.

To my therapist, Jamey. You have been so much more than a therapist to me the past seven years. You have truly helped me uncover my light on days it was buried beneath all the things I'd piled in the way. Thank you for being a true partner in my fight to live an authentic joy-filled life.

And finally, to my community. To every Instagram follower, Facebook community member, podcast listener, merchandise buyer, YouTube subscriber, and hopefully reader . . . I say this a million times because it's the truest thing I can say: if it weren't for you and your support of what I do I would not be in the place I am today. I am forever grateful for you. You are the reason I cried and spent thousands of hours writing and rewriting this book, because I always want to serve you with good content because you've given me this platform. Thank you for loving what I do, for watching my family grow, for buying and reading and listening and watching. I don't know what I did to deserve you guys. Thank you.

And to Jesus, Mary, and every saint I've prayed to for more than thirty years. Thank you for this life and for so many answered prayers, signs, and guidance. My faith has brought me here and I'll be forever grateful to have been brought up in a family of faith and to have it be such a huge part of my life.

And again, thank you to my reader. I thank you so much for taking time out of your one life to read my words. I'm forever grateful.

ABOUT THE AUTHOR

Mallory Ervin is a Kentucky-grown, Nashville-living dreamer who had a roundabout way of arriving at today. From her time in the Miss America pageant to being a three-time contestant on *The Amazing Race*, Mallory turned her passion for sharing her love of fashion, beauty, and life into a platform for impact. Today she runs a global lifestyle brand she founded in 2016; hosts the *Living Fully* podcast, where she encourages and inspires her dedicated following to seek joy and live fully; and appears across platforms ranging from Instagram to YouTube, sharing her life and message of living fully. She and her husband, Kyle, have two boys, Ford and Shepherd, and live in Nashville, Tennessee.

ABOUT THE TYPE

The text of this book was set in Janson, a typeface designed about 1690 by Nicholas Kis (1650–1702), a Hungarian living in Amsterdam, and for many years mistakenly attributed to the Dutch printer Anton Janson. In 1919, the matrices became the property of the Stempel Foundry in Frankfurt. It is an old-style book face of excellent clarity and sharpness. Janson serifs are concave and splayed; the contrast between thick and thin strokes is marked.